DRESS
YOUR TECH

DRESS
YOUR TECH

35 projects to customize
your phone, laptop,
tablet, camera, and more

Lucy Hopping

CICO BOOKS
LONDON NEW YORK

For Jude Alexander Gregg.

Published in 2015 by CICO Books
An imprint of Ryland Peters & Small Ltd
20–21 Jockey's Fields   341 E 116th St
London WC1R 4BW   New York, NY 10029

www.rylandpeters.com

10 9 8 7 6 5 4 3 2 1

Text © Lucy Hopping 2015
Design, photography, and artworks © CICO Books 2015

A CIP catalog record for this book is available from the
Library of Congress and the British Library.

ISBN: 978 1 78249 246 7

Printed in China

Editor: Marie Clayton
Design: Louise Turpin
Step artworks: Louise Turpin
Templates: Stephen Dew
Technique artworks: Stephen Dew and Kate Simunek
Photographer: Holly Jolliffe
Stylist: Joanna Thornhill

Editor: Carmel Edmonds
In-house designer: Fahema Khanam
Art director: Sally Powell
Production controller: Mai-Ling Collyer
Publishing manager: Penny Craig
Publisher: Cindy Richards

ACKNOWLEDGMENTS

Firstly, I would like to thank all at CICO; the
book looks absolutely wonderful and it has
been a complete pleasure working with you
all again. Special mention must go to Carmel,
Marie, and Louise who helped the
production of this book run smoothly,
despite the fact that I was nine months
pregnant when we started working on it
and gave birth halfway through!

I must also thank the Streatham Mums'
Network who rushed to my aid when
I needed old computer keyboards for one
of the projects. You saved me from buying
new ones!

My husband Jamie has been invaluable
throughout, looking after me, helping me
trawl the local charity shops for materials,
and looking after our baby so I could get
work done after he arrived. You have been
amazing as ever.

And finally, I must thank and dedicate this
book to my gorgeous baby boy Jude who
arrived on December 29, slightly earlier than
I expected, but was so well behaved that I
was able to get working again only days after
giving birth. You astonish and delight me
more each day darling boy, and I hope I can
get you to like arts and crafts just a little bit
as you grow up!

contents

introduction

Whether you are a technophobe or a techno whizz, this book will help you jazz up your gadgets so they stand out in a crowd. With mass-market phones, headphones, cameras, and tablets everywhere, you need to find a way to make them personal to you, and we hope that the 35 projects in this book will inspire you to create, upcycle, and decorate them so they are as cool as you are!

A wide selection of techniques is used throughout the book: sewing, crochet, knitting, weaving, and model making, to name but a few. Each project has a difficulty rating, so whether you are an experienced crafter or just starting out, I hope you can find inspiration to make something special.

The book is divided into three chapters, showing you how to Decorate Your Tech, Keep your Tech, and Protect your Tech. There is also a comprehensive techniques section to help with any sewing, knitting, or crochet queries you may have.

In the first chapter, Decorate Your Tech, we hope to inspire you to decorate your gadgets or office equipment so they are truly unique! Try upcycling a dull keyboard with washi tape, making a funky patchwork mouse mat and wrist rest, or crocheting foxy ears onto a pair of headphones, to mention just a few projects.

Keep Your Tech tackles the problem of storage and keeping things tidy. Keep your important files close with a beaded bracelet that cleverly incorporates a USB stick inside it, make a padded camera bag, or, if you enjoy exercising, sew an MP3 player armband.

The final chapter, Protect Your Tech, shows you clever ways to keep your tech protected from bumps and scratches. There are various ideas on how to decorate a phone case, make a mug-shaped felt case for your e-reader, or make a wipe-clean tablet stand that is ideal for using when you are cooking.

With varied projects that cover a wide selection of techniques and difficulties, there is something for everyone in this book. So grab your craft stash and your gadgets, and get crafting!

CHAPTER I

DECORATE
YOUR TECH

This section is crammed full of ideas to help you jazz up your gadgets and tech items and give them a new lease of life, using a variety of techniques. Projects include glittery phone chargers, clay USB sticks modeled into burgers, cupcakes, and sushi, and even a knitted cover for your mouse in the shape of a mouse! Follow the instructions to produce these fun creations that will make you the envy of all your friends.

picture bead headphones

This is the quickest and easiest way to brighten up your headphones! Try playing around with different color combinations and patterns for a variety of funky effects.

YOU WILL NEED
* **Assorted picture beads**
* **Small sharp scissors**
* **Pair of headphones**

1 Start by planning your design: arrange different colors and numbers of beads in a row until you are happy with the pattern.

2 Insert the tip of your scissors into the first bead and snip a slot into it.

3 Using a fingernail, gently open out the slot in the bead so you can clip it onto the wire of the headphone.

btw...

For a fun effect, try using a different pattern on the main wire than on the two thinner ones that lead to your ears.

4 Repeat along the whole length of the wires. Be careful not to pack the beads too tightly so your wires can still move and bend easily.

washi tape phone case covers

Jazz up your cellphone and make it as individual as you are with these fun washi tape phone cover cases. There are two options to try so get cutting and sticking to find your favorite!

YOU WILL NEED

* Clear plastic cellphone case cover for your model
* Thin white cardstock
* Pencil
* Assorted washi tapes
* Ruler
* Scissors
* Black fineliner pen
* Craft knife

Bunting design

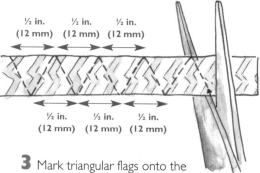

1 Draw around your phone case onto the cardstock, including any holes for the camera lens. Cut out the shape $1/16$ in. (2 mm) inside the outer line so that it will fit inside the case. Cut out the camera lens hole exactly on the line.

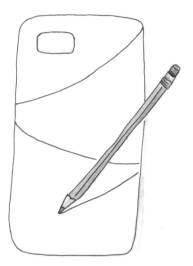

2 Turn the cardstock over and use a pencil to sketch out the hanging lines for the bunting flags, using the photograph as a guide for positioning.

½ in. (12 mm)   ½ in. (12 mm)   ½ in. (12 mm)

½ in. (12 mm)   ½ in. (12 mm)   ½ in. (12 mm)

3 Mark triangular flags onto the washi tape that are approximately ½ in. (12 mm) wide. Allow four per color so you can mix and match them. Cut the flags out.

4 Stick the flags along the bunting lines, arranging the different colors randomly. Outline each with a black fineliner pen so they stand out from the background. Draw the bunting lines in with the black pen.

5 Insert the cardstock piece into the phone case, then pop in your cellphone.

Stripy design

1 Cut strips of washi tape and lay them onto the outside of the phone case—try placing some strips next to each other and others overlapping, to create thicker and thinner lines of pattern. Cut the ends a little bit longer than the case sides.

2 Fold the ends of the tape up into the inside of the case for a neat finish. Using a craft knife, cut out the holes for the camera lens and any socket slots, folding the rough edges inside the case to neaten.

3 Insert your phone into the case.

fyi...

If your phone is colored, line the case with a piece of white cardstock so the design will look brighter.

These braided headphones will look as cool as the music you are listening to! Just use a couple of simple braiding techniques to cover the wires.

braided headphones

1 Choose two colors of floss (I started with mustard and dark green), fold both lengths in half, and tie them together onto the main part of the headphone cable, before it divides into two. You may find it helpful to tape the divider of the headphone cable onto a work surface to hold it in place while you're braiding.

SKILL LEVEL

YOU WILL NEED
* 8¾ yd (8 m) of embroidery floss in each of gray, coral, mustard, lime green, turquoise, dark green, and cream
* Set of ear-bud type headphones
* Tape (optional)
* Needle
* Scissors

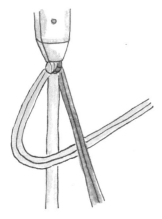

2 Starting with both mustard threads on the left and both green threads on the right, bring the mustard round and over the wire and then under the green.

3 Now bring the green thread under the wire and up through the loop of mustard on the left.

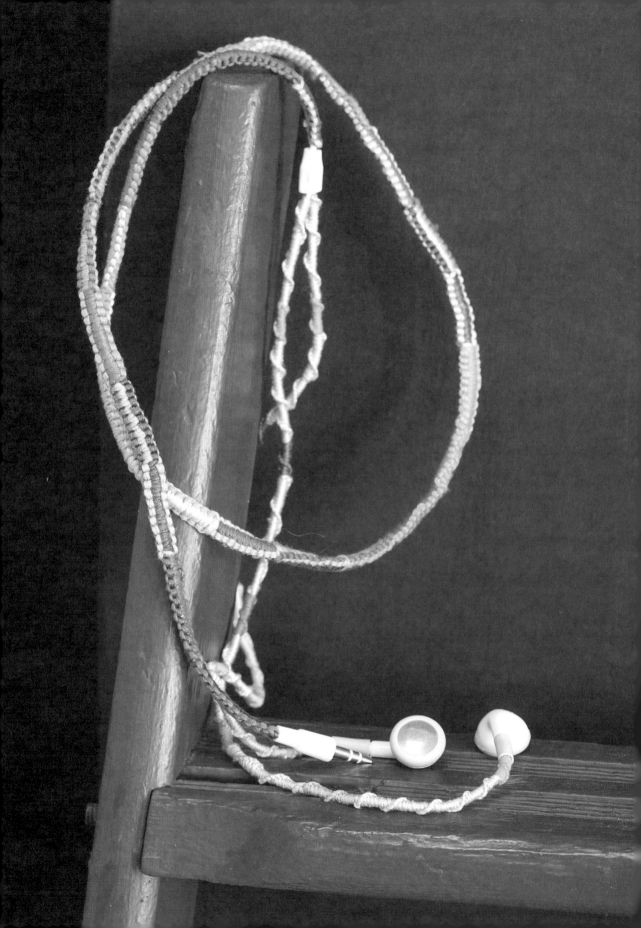

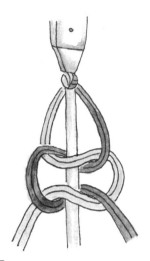

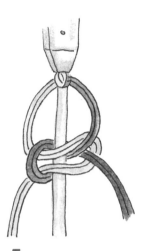

btw...

You can add beads to your headphone wires, too: thread a bead onto the threads you're working with, pull it up, and secure it in place with the next knot.

4 Repeat in the other direction so that the mustard thread now on the right goes over the wire and then under the green again, and the green thread goes under the wire and up through the loop of mustard on the right.

5 Pull the threads to tighten the knot.

6 Repeat steps 2–5 nine more times—you now have ten rows. Trim off the rest of the mustard, leaving a loose end of about ½ in. (1 cm). Now add coral: fold the coral in half to find the middle, then tie that onto the cable over the green and mustard threads. Work ten rows in green and coral by repeating steps 2–5, covering the ends of the mustard with the new knots.

7 For the next row, repeat steps 2–5 but reverse the colors for each step. So for example, in step 2, start with both green threads to the right and the coral on the left, then bring the green round and over the wire, then under the coral. Repeat nine more times.

8 Keep working bands of two different thread colors, changing the colors as as you like or using the photograph as a guide, until the whole wire is covered.

9 Using a needle, thread the last strands up through the braid to secure and trim off the ends.

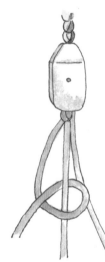

10 Now decorate the earbud cables. Take your first color (I used cream) and tie the end of the floss to one of the wires. Trim the short end. Starting with the floss on the left, take the floss over and round the wire, and then over itself. Repeat over and over to create a spiral effect. To change color, tie the new color around the cable and the previous floss. I used mainly cream floss, switching to a different color at intervals to create stripes. Thread the last threads up through the braid using the needle, and trim off any ends. Repeat with the second earbud cable.

glitter phone chargers

Glam up your phone charger with sparkly glitter patterns. I've used neon glitter but you could choose your favorite colors and patterns to make it personal to you.

SKILL LEVEL

YOU WILL NEED

* Phone charger for your model
* Pencil
* PVA glue
* Paintbrush
* Assorted neon glitter in yellow, pink, green, white, and black
* Clear nail varnish
* Masking tape

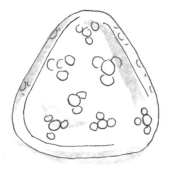

1 Use a pencil to lightly sketch out your design on top of the plug and on both sides of the connector. I chose zigzags for one of my chargers and leopard print for the other.

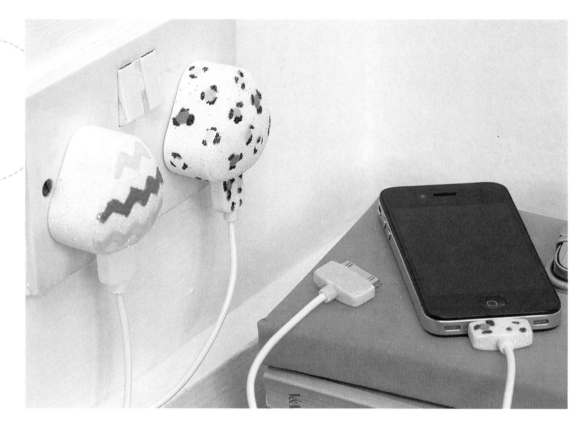

2 Carefully paint the first zigzag on the plug with PVA glue and then sprinkle with yellow glitter. Tap to remove the excess glitter. Paint the second zigzag stripe with PVA glue.

3 Sprinkle pink glitter on the second zigzag as before. On the third stripe use green glitter. Allow to dry.

4 Paint the remaining white sections on top of the plug with glue and cover with the white glitter. Allow to dry.

5 To seal the glitter, paint with a layer of clear nail varnish. Allow to dry.

6 Wrap the metal parts of the connector with masking tape to protect them. Paint one side of the connector with PVA and then sprinkle with glitter. Tap to remove the excess and allow to dry. Again, seal with nail varnish. Repeat on the other side.

7 For the leopard print design, follow the same steps, allowing each color to dry before applying the next to avoid mixing up the colors.

leather tassel phone charms

Make these fun and easy leather tassels in just a few steps! They look great as cellphone charms. Simply attach using a key ring and a phone charm loop (available online—it fits into the headphone socket).

SKILL LEVEL ✳ ✳ ✳

YOU WILL NEED

* 4 x 3 in. (10 x 7 cm) of cream leather
* 4 x 3 in. (10 x 7 cm) of green leather
* Pen and ruler
* Craft knife and cutting mat
* Superglue
* Stranded cotton embroidery floss in green, deep pink, and cream
* 3 in. (7.5 cm) of pink ribbon
* Needle
* Sewing thread

1 To make the green and cream tassel, cut a piece of leather 3 in. (7 cm) square from each color. Mark lines every 3/16 in. (5 mm) along the width of both pieces, stopping 1 in. (2.5 cm) from the top edge, then cut, using a craft knife and cutting mat.

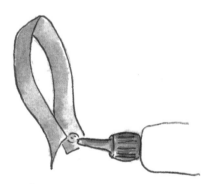

2 Cut another piece of leather 3/16 x 2 in. (5 mm x 5 cm) for the hanger and fold it in half lengthwise, wrong sides together. Stick the bottom ends together to make a loop and hold together until dry.

3 Place the green piece on top of the cream piece, both right side up, and stick together along the top uncut edge. On the wrong side put another line of glue along the top of the tassel and place the hanger at one end.

4 Roll up the tassel tightly and hold firmly until the glue is dry. Put to one side.

5 Make a braid approximately 3 in. (7.5 cm) long, using the stranded cotton, with one strand of green, one of deep pink, and one of cream.

fyi...

Try making layered and single color tassels with differently embroidered ribbons to add extra detail.

6 Sew the braid down the center of the length of ribbon, using sewing thread and small invisible stitches.

7 Glue the ribbon around the top of the tassel, folding one end under and overlapping the other for a neat finish. Attach the tassel to a phone charm loop and add to your cellphone.

foxy headphone covers

Perfect for keeping your ears cozy and warm, these crochet fox-ear covers are a great way to add character to your headphones. Adapt the colors and ear shape to make cat or bear ears, if you prefer.

SKILL LEVEL ✳ ✳ ✳

YOU WILL NEED

* ✳ 1¾ oz (50 g) of worsted (Aran) weight yarn in tweedy orange
* ✳ ⅜ oz (10 g) of worsted (Aran) weight yarn in black
* ✳ ⅜ oz (10 g) of worsted (Aran) weight yarn in cream
* ✳ US size 6 (4 mm) crochet hook
* ✳ Pair of headphones
* ✳ Yarn needle

GAUGE (TENSION)

* ✳ Gauge (tension) is not critical in this project

CROCHET TERMINOLOGY

US and UK crochet patterns share stitch names but these do not refer to the same stitches. This crochet pattern is written using US crochet terminology. See pages 118–120 for details of how to work each stitch. In this pattern, please note that:

Single crochet (US) = **double crochet** (UK)

I Using the tweedy orange yarn, make 3 chain stitches and join into a circle with a slip stitch. Work chain 1 and 6 single crochet stitches into the circle and join to the first stitch of the round to complete.

Round 1: Chain 1, work 2 single crochet into each stitch of the round. Slip stitch to the first stitch of the round to complete. (12 stitches)

Round 2: Chain 1, *work 2 single crochet into the first stitch, then a single crochet into the next stitch; repeat from * 5 more times and join to the first stitch of the round to complete. (18 stitches)

Round 3: Chain 1, *work 2 single crochet into the first stitch, then a single crochet into each of the next 2 stitches; repeat from * 5 more times and join to the first stitch of the round to complete. (24 stitches)

Round 4: Chain 1, *work 2 single crochet into the first stitch, then a single crochet into each of the next 3 stitches; repeat from * 5 more times and join to the first stitch of the round to complete. (30 stitches)

Round 5: Chain 1, *work 2 single crochet into the first stitch, then a single crochet into each of the next 4 stitches; repeat from * 5 more times and join to the first stitch of the round to complete. (36 stitches)

Round 6: Chain 1, *work 2 single crochet into the first stitch, then a single crochet into each of the next 5 stitches; repeat from * 5 more times and join to the first stitch of the round to complete. (42 stitches)

Round 7: Chain 1, *work 2 single crochet into the first stitch, then a single crochet into each of the next 6 stitches; repeat from * 5 more times and join to the first stitch of the round to complete. (48 stitches)

Round 8: Chain 1, *work 2 single crochet into the first stitch, then a single crochet into each of the next 7 stitches; repeat from * 5 more times and join to the first stitch of the round to complete. (54 stitches)

2 Check that the circle made will fit around the outside of the headphones—if not, work more rounds until it does.

3 Now begin the long piece in rows.
Row 1: Chain 1, work a single crochet into each of the next 6 stitches, turn. Repeat Row 1 until your piece is as long as the headphone section that goes over your head, approximately 75 rows. Cut the yarn and secure.

4 Make another circle as in steps 1–2 and then cut the yarn and secure, Stitch the second circle to the other end of the long piece.

5 Repeat steps 1–4 to make another piece that will go inside the headphones. The straight section will probably have to be a little shorter than on the outer piece, approximately 70 rows—it will depend on your headphones.

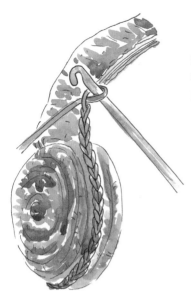

6 Place the two pieces right sides out and with the headphones sandwiched between. Join the pieces all around the edge with single crochet (or you can sew the pieces together) to completely encase the headphones.

7 To make the fox ears, using cream yarn make 6 chain stitches.
Row 1: Insert the crochet hook into the second stitch of the chain and work a single crochet stitch, work one single crochet in every stitch along the row, turn. (5 stitches)
Row 2: Chain 1, work a single crochet into each stitch, turn. (5 stitches)
Row 3: Chain 1, single crochet 2 stitches together, work a single crochet into each remaining stitch, turn. (4 stitches)
Row 4: Chain 1, single crochet 2 stitches together, work a single crochet into each remaining stitch, turn. (3 stitches)
Row 5: Chain 1, single crochet 2 stitches together, work a single crochet into the remaining stitch, turn. (2 stitches)
Row 6: Chain 1, single crochet 2 stitches together, cut the yarn, and thread it through the remaining stitch to secure.

8 Join in the tweedy orange yarn and work two rows of single crochet around the sides of the cream ear piece.

9 Join in the black yarn halfway up one side using a slip stitch, then work surface crochet (see page 120) around the top of the ear to half way down the other side. Finish with a slip stitch and secure.

10 Repeat steps 7–9 to make a second ear. Sew the ears on either side of the headphones toward the top, using the photograph as a guide.

touchscreen gloves

Sick of taking your gloves off in the cold weather to use your phone? No need now with these fab touchscreen gloves with clever conductive thread knitted into the fingertips. Magic!

YOU WILL NEED

* **Sirdar Heart & Sole 4-ply self-patterning sock yarn (75% wool, 25% nylon): 1 x 3½ oz/100 g ball (448 yd/410 m)**
* **Set of four US size 2 (2.75 mm) double-pointed needles**
* **Conductive thread**
* **Blunt-ended tapestry needle**
* **40 in. (100 cm) of narrow ribbon**

GAUGE (TENSION)

* **29 stitches and 38 rows to a 4-in. (10-cm) square on US size 2 (2.75 mm) double-pointed needles.**

FINISHED SIZE

* **Medium ladies' gloves, approx. 4 in. (10 cm) wide across the palm (excluding thumb) and 10 in. (25 cm) long**

1 Using three double-pointed needles, cast on 64 stitches. Join for working in the round, being careful not to twist your stitches. *Knit 1, purl 1; repeat from * to the end of the round. Mark the last stitch of the round and move the marker up every round. Repeat this round until the piece measures 3⅛ in. (8 cm) from the cast-on edge.

Round 1: *Knit 6, knit 2 together; repeat from * to the end of the round. (56 stitches)
Round 2: Knit.
Round 3: Knit 27, place a marker, make 1 left, knit 2, make 1 right, place a marker, knit 27 to the end of the round. (58 stitches)
Rounds 4 and 5: Knit.
Round 6: Knit 27 to the first marker, slip marker, make 1 left, knit to the next marker, make 1 right, slip marker, knit to the end of the round. (2 stitches increased)

2 *Repeat Rounds 4–6 seven more times. (74 stitches total, 20 stitches between markers) Knit 1 round.

3 **Next Round:** Knit to the first marker, remove marker, slip the next 20 stitches onto a stitch holder or scrap yarn for thumb, remove next marker then, with the wrong side facing you, cable cast on 4 stitches. Now with right side facing, join to the left side of the thumb gusset and continue to knit to the end of the round. (58 stitches)

btw...

For instructions on how to work the knitting stitches, see page 116–118.

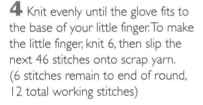

4 Knit evenly until the glove fits to the base of your little finger. To make the little finger, knit 6, then slip the next 46 stitches onto scrap yarn. (6 stitches remain to end of round, 12 total working stitches)

5 Next Round: With wrong side facing, cable cast on 3 stitches, then with right side facing and another double-pointed needle, knit 6 stitches to the end of the round. (15 working stitches)

Distribute the 15 stitches evenly onto three double-pointed needles, making sure the working yarn remains accessible at the end of a needle.

Knit evenly until the little finger reaches to right below the tip of your actual finger. When you try on the glove make sure that the base of the finger is snug inside the crook between your little and your ring finger.

Next Round: *Knit 1, knit 2 together; repeat from * to the end of the round. (10 stitches)

Next Round: *Knit 2 together; repeat from * to the end of the round. (5 stitches)

Cut the yarn and thread it through the remaining stitches.

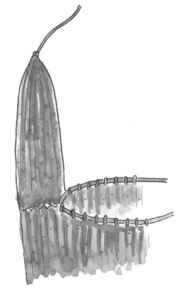

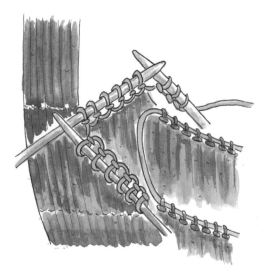

6 Cut the scrap yarn holding the remaining stitches and carefully slip 6 stitches from each end onto two double-pointed needles. (6 stitches on each needle, 12 stitches total)
Retie the scrap yarn.

7 Hold the glove so the little finger is on the right and the thumbhole is on the left, and rejoin the yarn—I changed to a turquoise section so the finger colors alternate. Knit 6 stitches from the front needle. With wrong side facing, cable cast on 3 stitches. Slip those 3 stitches onto another double-pointed needle.

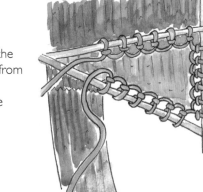

8 With right side facing, use the same needle to knit 3 stitches from the back needle. With another double-pointed needle, knit the last 3 stitches and then pick up 3 stitches from the base of the little finger.

9 Join for working in the round (18 stitches). Knit evenly until the ring finger fits to right below the tip of your actual ring finger.
Next Round: *Knit 1, knit 2 together; repeat from * to the end of the round. (12 stitches)
Next Round: *Knit 2 together; repeat from * to the end of the round. (6 stitches)
Cut the yarn and thread it through the remaining stitches.

10 Cut the scrap yarn and slip 8 stitches from each end onto two double-pointed needles. (8 stitches on each needle, 16 stitches total)
Retie the scrap yarn.
Hold the glove so that the little finger and ring finger are on the right and the thumbhole is on the left, and join the yarn—I changed to a lilac section so the finger colors alternate.
Knit 8 stitches from the front needle.

11 With wrong side facing, cable cast on 3 stitches. Slip those 3 stitches onto another double-pointed needle.
With right side facing, use the same needle to knit 4 stitches from the back needle.
With another double-pointed needle, knit the last 4 stitches and then pick up 3 stitches from the base of the ring finger.

12 Join for working in the round (22 stitches). Knit evenly until the middle finger fits to right below the tip of your actual middle finger.
Next Round: *Knit 1, knit 2 together; repeat from * to the last stitch, knit 1. (15 stitches)
Next Round: *Knit 2 together; repeat from * to the last stitch, knit 1. (8 stitches)
Cut the yarn and thread it through the remaining stitches.

13 Cut the scrap yarn and slip the remaining 18 stitches onto two double-pointed needles, 9 stitches each. Remove the scrap yarn.

Hold the glove so the other fingers are on the right and the thumbhole is on the left, and join a turquoise section of the yarn. Knit 7 stitches from the front needle.

With another double-pointed needle, knit the remaining 2 stitches from the front needle and use the same needle to knit 5 stitches from the back needle.

With another double-pointed needle, knit the remaining 4 stitches and pick up 3 stitches from the base of the middle finger.

Join for working in the round. (21 stitches)

Knit evenly until the index finger is up to your top finger joint. Join in the conductive thread and knit with this and the sock yarn together to the top of your finger, as for previous fingers.

Next Round: *Knit 1, knit 2 together; repeat from * to the end of the round. (14 stitches)

Next Round: *Knit 2 together; repeat from * to the end of the round. (7 stitches)

Cut the yarn and thread through the remaining stitches.

14 Slip the 20 stitches on hold for the thumb onto two double-pointed needles, 10 stitches each. Hold the glove so the fingers are on the right, and join a section of orange yarn.

Knit 8 stitches from the front needle.

With another double-pointed needle, knit the remaining 2 stitches from the front needle and use the same needle to knit 6 stitches from the back needle.

With another double-pointed needle, knit the remaining 4 stitches and pick up 3 stitches from the base of the thumb.

Join for working in the round. (23 stitches)

Knit evenly until the thumb fits to the top joint in your thumb. Join the conductive thread and knit with this and the sock yarn together to the top of your thumb, as in previous steps.

Next Round: *Knit 1, knit 2 together; repeat from * to the last 2 stitches, knit 2. (16 stitches)

Next Round: *Knit 2 together; repeat from * to the end of the round. (8 stitches)

Cut the yarn and thread it through the remaining stitches.

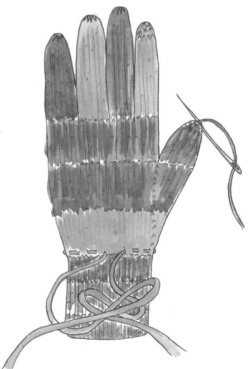

15 Use the tails at the bases of the fingers and thumb to carefully sew up any gaps and holes. Cut the length of ribbon in half. Thread a piece of ribbon through the gloves where the cuff and gusset meet and tie a bow. Make a second glove in the same way.

funky keyboard

Brighten up your desk space by decorating your computer keyboard with washi tape and metallic paint. It's so simple, but so effective!

SKILL LEVEL ✸ ✸ ✸

YOU WILL NEED

* **Keyboard**
* **Masking tape**
* **Silver spray paint**
* **Washi tape**
* **Scissors**
* **Dry-rub transfer letters**
* **Blunt stick or pencil**
* **Clear nail varnish**

1 Wrap the cord of the keyboard in masking tape—the spray paint will not stick to it so it is best to keep it clean. Take a picture of your keyboard so you know how to label each key after spray painting it.

2 Dust and clean the keyboard and then spray it with a thin layer of silver paint. Allow to dry then re-spray. Repeat until you have an even coat of paint on the front and back of the keyboard.

3 Once the keyboard is completely dry, cut pieces of washi tape in assorted designs and colors—the same size as the keyboard keys—and stick to the keys.

4 Add letters, numbers, and words to the relevant keys by rubbing the dry-rub letters down onto the keys using a blunt stick or pencil.

5 Paint each letter with a layer of clear nail varnish to seal. Remove the masking tape from the cord.

clay USB sticks

These look good enough to eat! Make your favorite snacks from oven-hardening modeling clay and add them to your USB storage sticks after baking for a crafty treat!

SKILL LEVEL ✳ ✳ ✳

YOU WILL NEED

* **USB sticks**
* **Oven-hardening modeling clay in white, yellow, red, cream, olive green, black, teal, pink, grass green, mustard, and brown**
* **Rolling pin or similar**
* **Knife or modeling tool**
* **Oven**
* **Superglue/glue gun (optional)**
* **Old toothbrush**

Sushi

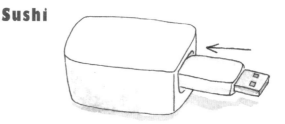

I Take a blob of white clay and wrap it around the USB stick loosely, avoiding the metal plug-in part. You may want to wiggle the USB stick around a little to make the hole slightly bigger so you can remove the stick easily before baking. Remove the USB key and set aside.

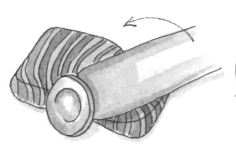

2 Roll out a piece of white clay and cut into thin strips approximately $1/16 \times 3/16$ in. (1×4 mm) then roll these slightly to make lots of grains of rice. Stick the grains around the sides and bottom of the white base blob.

3 Make the fish by mixing yellow and a little red to make a salmon-colored clay. Roll this out flat and add thin strips of cream clay to create a striped piece. With your finger rub the stripes together to create a salmon texture.

4 Cut the salmon into a rectangle and stick to the flat upper side of the white base. Mix the olive green and black clay to make a very dark green. Cut a long thin strip and wrap this around the center to complete your sushi design.

5 Bake the sushi design in the oven according to the instructions on the clay packet. Once it has cooled, push the USB stick back into the hole.

Cupcake

1 Repeat Step 1 of the sushi using teal clay and making the shape more circular with ribs like a cupcake case.

2 Make a dome shape using cream clay on top of the case. Roll out a piece of pink clay to make the icing and decorate with sprinkles made from white, yellow, and green clay.

3 Bake as for the sushi and insert the USB stick when cooled.

Hamburger

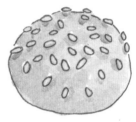

1 Mix the mustard clay with a little cream clay to make a bun-colored clay. Divide in two and make one into a round disc and the other into a dome shape. This will form the top and bottom of the bun. Add dots of cream clay for sesame seeds.

2 Roll a piece of yellow clay out and make it into a square, then cut out a rectangle in the middle the same size as the USB stick. Layer this on top of the bun base to make the cheese slice.

3 Shape a piece of brown clay into a burger and use an old toothbrush to create the texture round the sides. Again cut out the center and layer on top of the cheese.

4 Make a lettuce leaf from grass green clay, cutting a ragged edge to the leaf. Again cut out a rectangle at the center and place on the burger. Make little wedges of red clay for the tomatoes and place on the lettuce.

5 Complete by adding the bun top. Bake as for the sushi and insert the USB stick when cooled.

crochet camera buddies

These fun crochet characters are ideal for distracting the kids so you can capture the perfect photograph! Simply slip one on your camera lens—try the designs below or adapt to make your own.

YOU WILL NEED

* ¾ oz (20 g) of light worsted (DK) cotton yarn in each of gray, coral, turquoise, green, mustard, and orange
* ⅜ oz (10 g) of light worsted (DK) cotton yarn in each of black, cream, and brown
* US size E4 (3.5 mm) crochet hook
* 3 elastic hair bands
* Scissors
* Needle
* Cardstock
* Gray felt
* Thread

GAUGE (TENSION)

* Gauge (tension) is not critical in this project

FINISHED SIZE

* Central hole is 1½ in. (4 cm) diameter, but this stretches to approximately 3⅛ in. (8 cm)

Rabbit

❚ First make the face.

Round 1: Using gray yarn, work 36 single crochet around one of the hair bands.

Round 2: Chain 2, *work 2 half-double crochet into the first stitch, then a half-double crochet into each of the next 2 stitches; repeat from * 11 more times and join to the first stitch of the round to complete. (48 stitches)

Round 3: Chain 2, *work 2 half-double crochet into the first stitch, then a half-double crochet into each of the next 3 stitches; repeat from * 11 more times and join to the first stitch of the round to complete. (60 stitches)

Round 4: Chain 2, *work 2 half-double crochet into the first stitch, then a half-double crochet into each of the next 4 stitches; repeat from * 11 more times and join to the first stitch of the round to complete. (72 stitches.)

CROCHET TERMINOLOGY

US and UK crochet patterns share stitch names but these do not refer to the same stitches.

This crochet pattern is written using US crochet terminology. See pages 118–120 for details of how to work each stitch. In this pattern, please note that:

Single crochet (US) = **double crochet** (UK)
Half-double crochet (US) = **half-treble crochet** (UK)
Double crochet (US) = **treble crochet** (UK)
Treble (US) = **double treble crochet** (UK)

Round 5: Chain 2, *work 2 half-double crochet into the first stitch, then a half-double crochet into each of the next 5 stitches; repeat from * 11 more times and join to the first stitch of the round to complete. (84 stitches).

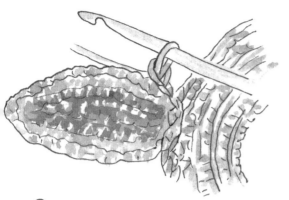

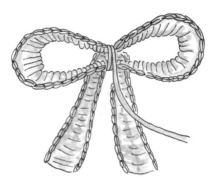

2 Now make the ears.

Join the coral yarn and make a chain of 13 stitches.

Row 1: Skip 1 chain, then work 2 single crochet, 2 half-double crochet, 2 double crochet, 1 treble crochet, 2 double crochet, 2 half-double crochet, 2 single crochet.

Row 2: Chain 1, turn and work single crochet around the edge, working 3 single crochet at the center.

Fasten off the yarn.

Row 3: Join the gray yarn and work 2 rows of single crochet around the edges of the coral inner ear, with 3 single crochet at the center.

Fasten off the yarn, leaving a long end. Catch down row-ends.

Miss 15 stitches and join in coral yarn. Repeat to make the second ear.

3 Now make the bow.

Make a chain of 20 stitches in turquoise yarn, join to the first stitch to create a circle.

Round 1: Work 2 single crochet, 3 half-double crochet, 8 double crochet, 3 half-double crochet, 4 single crochet, 3 half-double crochet, 8 double crochet, 3 half-double crochet, and 2 single crochet into the circle. Slip stitch to the first stitch, cut the end leaving a 20 in. (50 cm) tail and thread the end through the last stitch.

Make the dangling ends:

Make a chain of 26 stitches in turquoise yarn.

Row 1: 1 double crochet in the 3rd chain from the hook, 1 double crochet in each of the next 7 stitches, 1 half-double crochet in each of the next 2 stitches, 1 single crochet in each of the next 4 stitches, 1 half-double crochet in each of the next 2 stitches, 1 double crochet in each of the next 7 stitches, chain 2 and slip stitch into the last stitch. Fasten off the yarn.

Assemble the bow by holding it with the single crochet pinched together in the center. Attach the dangling ends by winding the long yarn tail around the two until they are securely joined. Tie firmly and sew in place.

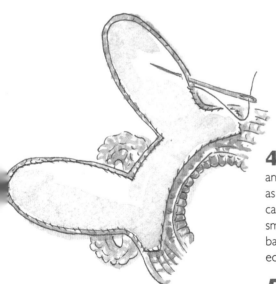

4 To stiffen the ears so they stand up, draw around the ears and top of the face onto the cardstock and cut out. Use this as a template to cut out the backing from gray felt. Trim the cardstock ears down by 1/4 in. (5 mm) all round, so they're smaller than the felt ears. Place the cardstock shape on the back of the rabbit and add the felt on top. Sew around the edge of the felt to secure both card and felt in place.

5 Using surface crochet (see page 120) or chain stitch (see page 115), work three whiskers on each side of the face.

Frog

1 **To make the body,** repeat Step 1 of the Rabbit using green yarn.
Fasten off the yarn.

2 **Now make the right leg.**
Turn the work and rejoin the yarn 20 stitches from the fastened-off yarn end. Work the following: 2 slip stitches, 2 single crochet, 2 half-double crochet, 2 double crochet, 8 trebles, 1 double crochet, 1 half-double crochet, 1 single crochet, 1 slip stitch.
Chain 1, turn, then work 1 slip stitch, 1 single crochet, 1 half-double crochet, 1 double crochet, 3 trebles, 2 trebles into each of the next 2 stitches, 3 trebles, 2 double crochet, 2 half-double crochet, 2 single crochet, 2 slip stitches.

3 **Make the foot.**
Make a chain of 6 stitches, 1 single crochet into each stitch along the chain (5 stitches) and then slip stitch into the body. Repeat 2 more times so there are 3 toes.
Fasten off the yarn.

4 Miss 18 stitches after foot and with right side facing, join yarn to next stitch. Repeat steps 2 and 3 on the other side of the body to make the left leg.

5 **Now make the eyes.**
Round 1: Make a chain of 4 stitches with the black yarn, join into a circle with a slip stitch and then work 6 single crochet into the circle, join to the first stitch with a slip stitch, cut and secure yarn.
Round 2: Join the cream yarn and work 2 single crochet into each stitch. (12 stitches)
Round 3: Join the green yarn and work 2 half-double crochet into 1 stitch, then 1 half-double crochet into the next. Repeat around the round. (18 stitches)
Repeat to make a second eye.

6 Stitch the eyes to the frog's face.

7 Using surface crochet (see page 120) or chain stitch (see page 115), work a black mouth on the frog.

Lion

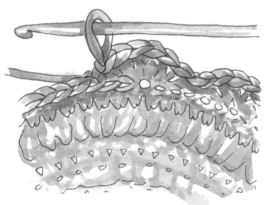

1 **To make the body,** repeat Step 1 of the Rabbit using mustard yarn. Do not work the fifth round.

Change to orange yarn, chain 1, *work 2 single crochet into the first stitch, then a single crochet into each of the next 5 stitches; repeat from * 11 more times and join to the first stitch of the round to complete. (84 stitches)

Chain 3, work 5 double crochet into the same stitch, work a slip stitch into the 3rd stitch from the scallop. Make another scallop by working 6 double crochet into the 3rd stitch from the slip stitch. Repeat all around the outside of the face. Fasten off the yarn.

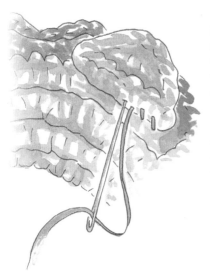

2 **To make the ears:**
Row 1: Using the mustard yarn, make a chain of 9 stitches, then work 1 half-double crochet into third chain and 1 half-double crochet into each of next 6 stitches. (7 stitches)
Row 2: Chain 2, turn, half-double crochet 2 together, 3 half-double crochet, half-double crochet 2 together. (5 stitches)
Row 3: Chain 1, turn, single crochet 2 together, 1 single crochet, single crochet 2 together. (3 stitches)
Secure yarn and sew to the head. Repeat to make the second ear.

3 **Now make the eyes.**
Repeat Step 5 of the Frog with brown and cream yarn. Do not work the third round of the eye. Stitch to the lion. Repeat to make the second eye.

4 Complete by working surface crochet (see page 120) or chain stitch (see page 115) with the brown yarn to make a mouth.

patchwork mouse mat and wrist rest

Show off your favorite fabrics with this matching mouse mat and wrist rest. Simply stitch the fabrics together using the paper patchwork technique before finishing.

SKILL LEVEL ✳ ✳ ✳

YOU WILL NEED

* Mouse mat
* Pencil
* Sheets of paper
* Ruler
* Scissors
* Assorted pieces of fabric around 6 in. (15 cm) square
* Needle and thread
* 9 x 10 in. (22.5 x 25 cm) of Bondaweb
* Red embroidery floss
* 40 in. (100 cm) of bias binding
* Superglue
* Crochet doily
* Bag of rice

Mouse mat

1 Draw around the mouse mat onto one of the sheets of paper and then divide the paper mouse mat into squares at least 2 in. (5 cm) in size. Cut out all the paper squares.

2 Cut squares of fabric big enough to cover your squares of paper plus a seam allowance. Place a square of paper onto the wrong side of each piece of fabric and fold over the seam allowance. Baste (tack) in place.

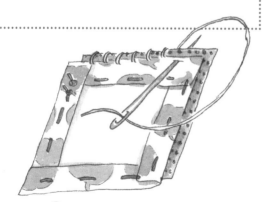

4 Repeat to make five lines of four squares, then sew the lines together in the same way so that your mouse mat shape is recreated in fabric.

3 Place two of the fabric squares right sides together and overstitch together along one side.

5 Remove all the basting (tacking) stitches and paper pieces and iron flat. Iron the Bondaweb onto the back of the patchwork.

6 Peel off the paper backing of the Bondaweb and iron the patchwork onto the mouse mat. Round off the corners with scissors to match the mat.

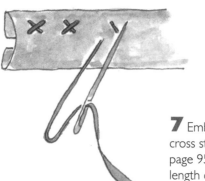

7 Embroider red cross stitches (see page 95) along the length of the bias binding, but only on one side.

8 Stitch the cross-stitched edge of the bias binding around the edge of the mouse mat using tiny invisible slipstitches.

9 Fold the other edge of the bias binding over to the back of the mouse mat, enclosing the raw edge and folding the raw end under. Use superglue to fix in place.

Wrist rest

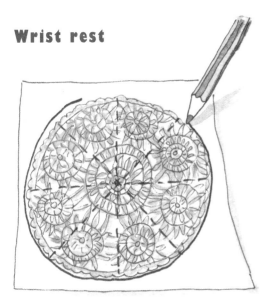

1 Draw around your crochet doily (mine was 11 in./27 cm in diameter) onto another piece of paper. Divide the paper circle into eight wedges and cut them out.

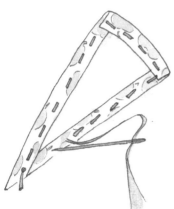

2 Cut pieces of fabric larger than the paper wedges by the width of a seam allowance all around. Place a segment of paper onto the wrong side of each piece of fabric and fold over the seam allowance. Baste in place all around.

3 Place two wedges right sides together and stitch together as with the mouse mat. Repeat to make up the circle in fabric.

4 Remove the basting and the paper pieces and iron the circle flat.

5 Fold the circle in half right sides together and stitch around the curved edge, leaving a small gap in the seam.

6 Turn inside out and fill with rice—approximately 2 cups will be enough. Slipstitch the gap in the seam closed.

7 Wrap the patchwork pillow in the doily and sew around the edges to keep it in place—I used blanket stitch (see page 115) around the scalloped edges.

knitted mouse cover

YOU WILL NEED

* ⅞ oz (25 g) of light worsted (DK) cotton yarn in gray
* ⅜ oz (10 g) of light worsted (DK) cotton yarn in pink
* Scraps of black and cream yarn
* Pair of US size 4 (3.5 mm) knitting needles
* Yarn needle
* Superglue

GAUGE (TENSION)

* Gauge (tension) is not critical in this project

FINISHED SIZE

* Fits a mouse approximately 2⅜ x 4½ in. (6 x 11.5 cm) and 1½ in. (4 cm) deep

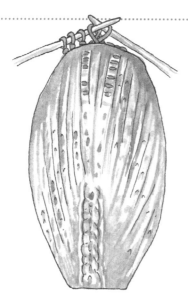

Turn your mouse into a mouse! This cute knitted cover will give your desk a bit of personality and fun.

1 Using the gray yarn cast on 7 stitches.

Row 1: Knit.

Row 2: Purl.

Row 3: Knit 2, knit in front and back of next stitch, knit in front and back of following stitch, knit 3. (9 stitches)

Row 4: Purl.

Rows 5–26: As Rows 3–4, continuing to increase the number of knit stitches by 1 at each end until you have 31 stitches on your needle.

Rows 27–38: Repeat Rows 1–2.

Row 39: Knit 5, slip 1 stitch, knit 1 stitch, pass slipped stitch over, knit 5, slip 1 stitch, knit 1 stitch, pass slipped stitch over, knit 3, knit 2 together, knit 5, knit 2 together, knit 5. (27 stitches)

Row 40: Purl.

Row 41: Knit 4, slip 1 stitch, knit 1 stitch, pass slipped stitch over, knit 4, slip 1 stitch, knit 1 stitch, pass slipped stitch over, knit 3, knit 2 together, knit 4, knit 2 together, knit 4. (23 stitches)

Row 42: Purl.

Row 43: Knit 3, slip 1 stitch, knit 1 stitch, pass slipped stitch over, knit 3, slip 1 stitch, knit 1 stitch, pass slipped stitch over, knit 3, knit 2 together, knit 3, knit 2 together, knit 3. (19 stitches)

Row 44: Purl.

Row 45: Knit 2, slip 1 stitch, knit 1 stitch, pass slipped stitch over, knit 2, slip 1 stitch, knit 1 stitch, pass slipped stitch over, knit 3, knit 2 together, knit 2, knit 2 together, knit 2. (15 stitches)

Row 46: Purl.

Row 47: Knit 1, slip 1 stitch, knit 1 stitch, pass slipped stitch over, knit 1, slip 1 stitch, knit 1 stitch, pass slipped stitch over, knit 3, knit 2 together, knit 1, knit 2 together, knit 1. (11 stitches)

Row 48: Purl.

Row 49: Slip 1 stitch, knit 1 stitch, pass slipped stitch over, slip 1 stitch, knit 1 stitch, pass slipped stitch over, knit 3, knit 2 together, knit 2 together. (7 stitches)

Row 50: Purl.

Bind (cast) off.

2 To make the ears, cast on 3 stitches.
Row 1: Knit in front and back of next stitch, knit 2.
(4 stitches)
Row 2: Knit in front and back of next stitch, purl 3.
(5 stitches)
Rows 3–6: Repeat Rows 1 and 2, increasing by 1 st
each time until you have 9 stitches on your needle.
Row 7: Knit.
Row 8: Purl.
Row 9: Slip 1 stitch, knit 1 stitch, pass slipped stitch
over, knit 5, knit 2 together. (7 stitches)
Row 10: Slip 1 stitch, knit 1 stitch, pass slipped stitch
over, purl 3, purl 2 together. (5 stitches)
Cut yarn and thread through all the remaining
stitches.
Sew to the face of the mouse. Repeat to make
a second ear.

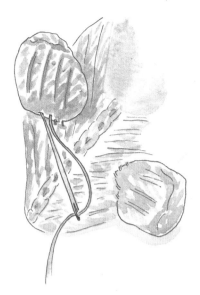

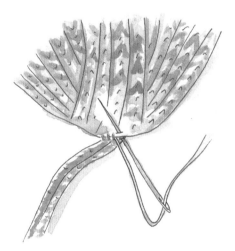

3 To make the tail, cast on 4
stitches using the pink yarn. Work
rows of stockinette (stocking)
stitch (alternate rows knit and
purl) until your tail measures
approximately 5 in. (12.5 cm).
Sew onto the back of the mouse.

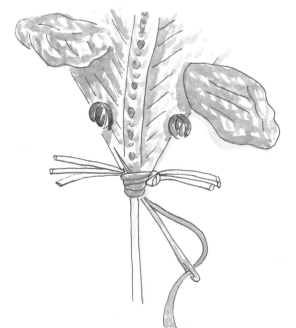

4 Complete your mouse by sewing a large French knot (see page 115) in black yarn for each eye, a nose in satin stitch (see page 114) using pink yarn and adding whiskers using three short lengths of cream yarn knotted together and threaded through near the nose. Note that I have threaded the cable from the mouse through the nose area and stitched around to secure it.

5 To attach your knitting to the mouse, apply a thin layer of superglue around the outer edges of the mouse, except along the top edge where the buttons are. Press the edges of your knitting to the glue. Add a dot of glue to the nose to fix it in place on the cable.

laptop desk

This go-anywhere study space keeps you comfortable with its cushioned base and sturdy work surface.

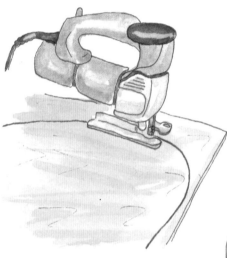

SKILL LEVEL

YOU WILL NEED

* 16 x 24 in. (40 x 60 cm) of ⅜ in. (10 mm) thick **MDF** sheet
* Pencil
* Small saw or jigsaw
* Green spray paint
* 16 x 24 in. (40 x 60 cm) of 3 in. (7.5 cm) thick upholstery foam
* Craft knife
* 30 x 36 in. (75 x 90 cm) of vintage floral fabric
* Scissors
* Needle and thread
* Staple gun
* 2 yd (2 m) of pompom trim

1 Draw a rectangle 16 in (40 cm) deep and 20 in. (50 cm) wide onto the MDF sheet and then mark a semi circle cutout at the center of one long side, using the photo as a guide. Round off all the corners. Cut out the shape using a saw or jigsaw.

2 Spray paint the MDF on one side. Allow to dry, and then repeat to add another coat. Allow to dry thoroughly.

3 Use the craft knife to cut a piece of upholstery foam exactly the same size and shape as the MDF piece. Cut a piece of fabric the same shape but with an extra ³/₈ in (1 cm) all around as a seam allowance.

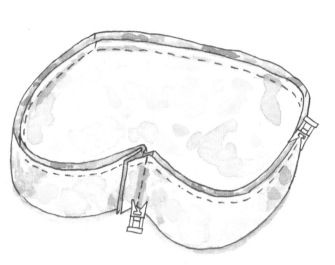

4 Cut strips 4 in. (40 cm) deep across the width of the remaining fabric. Join the short ends right side together to make one strip at least 78 in. (195 cm) long. Pin this right sides together around the edge of the main fabric piece, and then sew together with a $^3/_8$ in. (1 cm) seam allowance. Sew the two ends of the fabric together in the same way.

5 Turn the fabric right side out and place the upholstery foam inside it.

6 Fold the raw edges of the fabric over and place the MDF sheet on top. Using the staple gun attach the folded fabric edge to the edge of the MDF sheet all around.

7 To hide the staples, sew the pompom trim along the top of the fabric where it joins the MDF, using small stitches.

CHAPTER 2

KEEP
YOUR TECH

With all the wires, plugs, and bits and pieces that come with your gadgets these days, you need a way to store and tidy them that still looks stylish. Upcycling is still a huge craze and this chapter has lots of ideas that will inspire you to create new items from old objects. Learn how to make a phone charger tidy from a lotion bottle, a laptop case from an upcycled vintage book, and a hair tool tidy from a drainage pipe—as well as projects made from new materials.

phone charger tidy

Keep things tidy with this clever cellphone charger holder, which is made from a recycled lotion bottle. Decorate using decoupage papers and gems for a modern look.

SKILL LEVEL ✳ ✳ ✳

YOU WILL NEED

* Large lotion or bubble bath bottle
* Cellphone charger
* Permanent marker pen
* Craft knife
* Cutting mat
* Assortment of pretty decoupage papers
* Decoupage or PVA glue
* Paintbrush
* Flat-backed gems
* Glue gun/superglue

I Make sure the base of the bottle is big enough to hold your cellphone. Mark out where you want to cut your bottle at the front and back. To get the right size and shape for the opening in the back, draw around the plug of your charger.

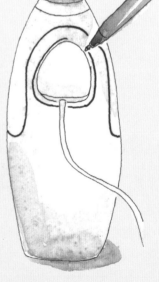

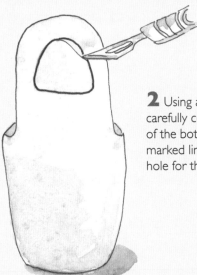

2 Using a craft knife, carefully cut away the top of the bottle along the marked line. Cut out the hole for the plug.

3 Cut the decoupage papers into small squares and stick them to the bottle using decoupage or PVA glue. I used one design for the inside, one for the outside and edged around the top in a third. You could also just layer the squares at random, but make sure the whole of the bottle is completely covered.

4 Set aside and allow the glue to dry completely.

5 Using a glue gun or superglue, attach a row of gems to cover the join where the main paper and edge papers meet, both to neaten the join and add a bit of glitz!

USB key ring case

Keep your important work, favorite photos, and music close by at all times with this USB key ring case. Use contrasting fabrics for a funky effect.

1 Cut two template A pieces (see page 121) from blue fabric. Iron all edges on both pieces over to the wrong side by ¼ in. (5 mm).

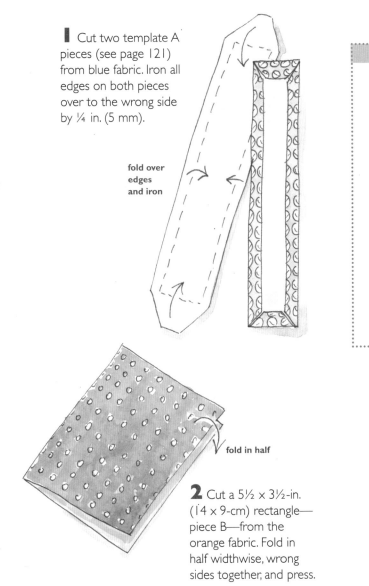

fold over edges and iron

fold in half

see page 121

2 Cut a 5½ x 3½-in. (14 x 9-cm) rectangle—piece B—from the orange fabric. Fold in half widthwise, wrong sides together, and press.

3 Concertina the edges of piece B as shown in the illustration and then press the folds flat.

4 Place the two A pieces wrong sides together. Turn the folded piece B over and slide the two raw edges between the layers of A on either side, approximately 1 in. (2.5 cm) up from the bottom edge. Pin in place on either side through all layers of A and the bottom fold of piece B only.

5 Holding the upper folds on piece B out of the way, sew along the two long sides of piece A—making sure you only catch the bottom folded edge of the B piece on each side—and across the top end of piece A.

6 Thread the split ring onto the unstitched end of piece A, fold over the raw edge and then fold over the end again and bring up to overlap the bottom of piece B. Flatten the loop and then sew across the fold through all layers, closing the bottom of the pocket for the USB at the same time.

fold over
split ring
and sew

7 Sew one half of the snap fastener onto the bottom of the pocket and the matching half onto the other end of the key ring.

hot air balloon headphone case

Keep your headphones safe and sound in this little case rather than screwed up in the bottom of your purse. They also have a handy clip to attach to a key ring or purse loop.

1 Using the templates on page 125, cut out one front panel (A) and two back panels (B) from teal felt. Cut one center panel (C) from cream felt.

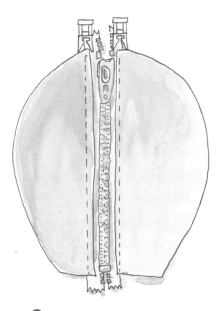

2 With the zipper right side up, sew the two back panels to the tape on either side of the teeth using a sewing machine.

SKILL LEVEL ✳ ✳ ✳

YOU WILL NEED

- ✳ **6 in. (15 cm) square of teal felt**
- ✳ **8 x 6 in. (20 x 15 cm) square of cream felt**
- ✳ **Scissors**
- ✳ **4 in. (10 cm) zipper**
- ✳ **Sewing machine and thread**
- ✳ **5 in. (12.5 cm) square of cotton fabric in each of three designs**
- ✳ **Small sharp embroidery scissors**
- ✳ **Scraps of shiny blue fabric**
- ✳ **Sequins**
- ✳ **Sewing needle**
- ✳ **Lobster clasp clip**

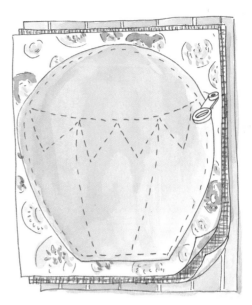

3 Layer the three squares of patterned fabric all right side up. Add the teal front panel on top. Stitch the lines onto your hot air balloon, using the illustration as a guide. If you prefer you can make your own design, using a free machine embroidery foot on your sewing machine to get the detail you require.

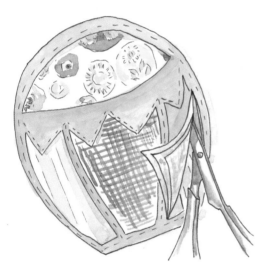

4 Using the small sharp embroidery scissors, cut away layers of fabric to reveal different patterns behind. I cut only the felt layer away for the top section of the balloon, the felt and the top layer of fabric only for the central part of the balloon, and the felt and the two upper layers of fabric to reveal the third fabric for the sides.

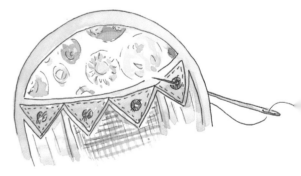

5 Cut small triangles of the shiny blue fabric and sew them over the felt triangles in the design to make a line of bunting. Stitch a sequin into the center of each triangle.

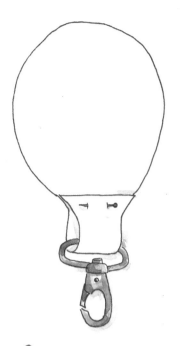

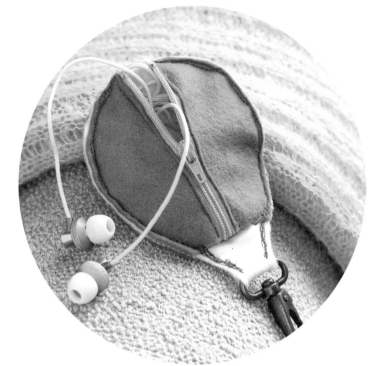

6 Thread the lobster clasp clip onto the bottom tab on the cream center panel, then fold the tab upward and pin.

7 With right sides out, pin the front piece and zippered back piece on either side of the cream piece. Tuck the zipper tape ends away between the layers.

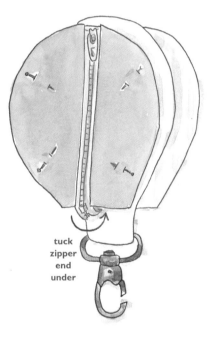

tuck zipper end under

8 Using the sewing machine, stitch together all the layers around the edge of the balloon. Add a few lines of stitching to represent the strings to the basket (or clip) of the design. Trim around the edge to neaten if necessary.

woven camera strap

Weave a bright and colorful camera strap to personalize your camera. If you don't want to weave the strap, replace with a strip of colorful contrasting fabric instead.

YOU WILL NEED

* 36 x 4 in. (90 x 10 cm) of thick mountboard
* Ball of colored twine
* Cotton tapestry yarn in green, cream, red, mustard, and blue
* Blunt-ended needle
* Scissors
* Interfacing or felt
* Patterned cotton fabric
* Sewing needle
* Sewing thread
* Sewing machine and white thread
* 2 lobster clasp clips, 1½ in. (4 cm) in size

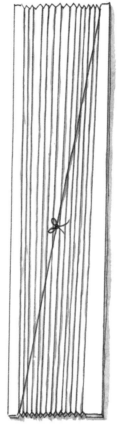

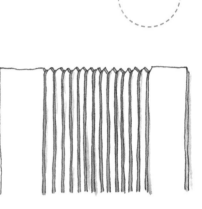

1 Make a loom from the piece of mountboard by making 14 notches ¼ in. (5 mm) apart along the top and bottom short edges of the strip. Wrap the twine around the notches to create the warp threads.

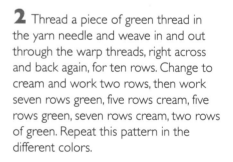

2 Thread a piece of green thread in the yarn needle and weave in and out through the warp threads, right across and back again, for ten rows. Change to cream and work two rows, then work seven rows green, five rows cream, five rows green, seven rows cream, two rows of green. Repeat this pattern in the different colors.

3 Continue until the woven piece measures approximately 32 in. (80 cm).

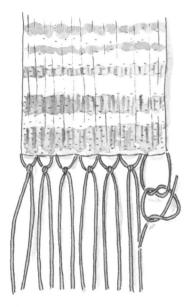

4 Cut the back strings so the weaving is free from the loom and tie pairs of strings together tightly at each end to secure and keep the weaving together. Trim the ends to 4 in. (10 cm).

5 Thread in all the other different color thread ends along the length of the weaving and press flat.

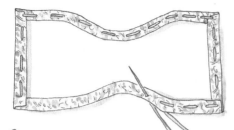

6 Using the small template on page 121, cut two interfacing or felt shapes. Use the large template to cut two fabric shapes. Place an interfacing/felt piece in the center of each fabric piece, fold over the edges and baste (tack) in place.

7 Sew around the edge of each fabric piece using the sewing machine and then remove the basting (tacking) stitches.

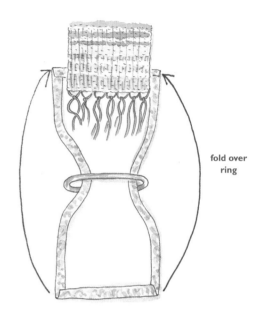

fold over ring

8 Thread the D-ring on one of the lobster clasp clips onto one fabric shape. Place one end of the woven piece on the inside of the fabric piece, arranging the warp ends to fill one half of the fabric (this will create a strong base for the fabric to sew to). Fold the other half over.

9 Using the sewing machine stitch around to join together, then stitch a box and cross pattern to strengthen the ends.

10 Repeat steps 8–9 on the other end to complete your strap.

vintage book laptop case

Make a quirky laptop case from a vintage book to keep it safe and protected against bumps. You will need to scour thrift stores and yard sales for a suitably sized hardback book cover but it's worth the hunt!

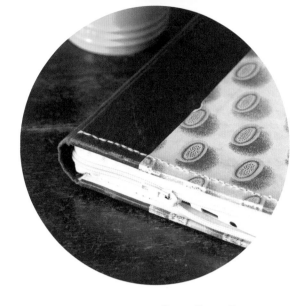

SKILL LEVEL

SKILL LEVEL

YOU WILL NEED

* Hardcover book bigger than your laptop
* Pencil and ruler
* Electric drill with $^5/_8$ in. (1.5 mm) bit
* Needle
* Strong sewing thread
* Zipper to go round three sides of the book
* Stranded cotton embroidery floss
* 15 x 25 in. (37.5 x 62.5 cm) of fleece

1 Remove the pages of the book so that just the outer hard cover remains.

2 Using the pencil and ruler, measure in $^3/_8$ in. (1 cm) in from the outer edge of the book cover and then mark along at this position every $^1/_4$ in. (5 mm) all around the outside.

3 Using the drill, make a hole right through the cover at each mark all around the edges.

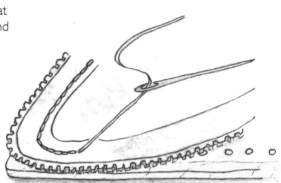

4 Using the strong sewing thread and needle, sew one side of the zipper tape right side down around the inside edge of one half of the book cover from the top of the spine to the bottom of the spine, stitching through the holes in the book. Sew the second side of the tape in the same way to the other half of the cover with the zipper open—close it at intervals during the stitching to ensure that it all still matches up.

5 Repeat step 4 with the stranded cotton to add extra strength and fill the drilled holes to make them look neater.

6 To make the inside of the case neater and add extra protection, line it with a piece of fleece fabric. Cut the fleece the same size as the book opened out flat, including the spine.

7 Lay the fleece over the inside of the book. Turning the edge under by ³/₈ in. (1 cm) as you go, slipstitch the folded edge to the zipper tape near the teeth, using strong sewing thread.

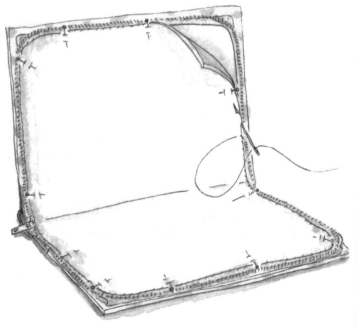

owl remote control pillow

That's a wise idea—make a pocket pillow in the shape of an owl
to hold all your remote controls so they don't get lost down the sofa!

SKILL LEVEL

YOU WILL NEED

* Scissors
* 15 x 40 in. (37.5 x 100 cm) of
  teal tweed
* 7 x 12 in. (17.5 x 30 cm) of duck
  egg blue spotty fabric
* White and teal sewing thread
* Sewing machine
* 12 x 24 in. (30 x 60 cm) of orange
  and pink floral fabric
* Sewing needle
* 5 x 12 in. (12.5 x 30 cm) of orange
  dotty fabric
* Felt in olive green, cream, black,
  and yellow
* Fiberfill stuffing

1 Using the templates on pages 122–123, cut out two
owl shaped cushion pieces for the front and back and
a base piece from the teal tweed fabric.

2 Fold the duck egg blue fabric in half wrong sides
together and place the pocket piece template on the fold
as marked. Cut out and press. Topstitch along the folded
edge and then put to one side.

2 in.
(5cm)

3 Fold the
pink and orange
floral fabric in half and use
the template to cut out two
pairs of wing pieces. Place the first
pair right sides together and sew around the
edge with a 3/8 in. (1 cm) seam allowance,
leaving a gap in the seam 2 in. (5 cm) long.

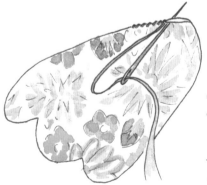

4 Turn the wing right side out, press flat and slipstitch the
opening closed. Repeat with the other two wing pieces.

5 Use the templates to cut out an inner eye patch from
the orange dotty fabric, a scalloped eye patch from the
olive felt, outer eyes from the cream and inner eyes from
the black felt, and a beak from the yellow felt.

6 Machine stitch the face pieces onto the front of one of the owl shapes, following the photograph as a guide. Add the pocket and stitch down it twice to make three equal sections.

7 Place the base piece of the cushion right sides together to the front of the owl and machine stitch in place along one side.

2 in. (5cm)

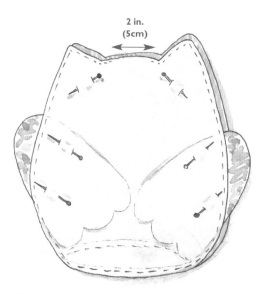

8 Pin the wings in place on either side on top of the front, so the wings lie over the body. Place the back of the owl onto the front and base piece, right sides together, and pin. Sew it around the body and base piece, leaving a 2 in. (5 cm) gap at the top.

9 Turn the owl right side out, fill fairly firmly with stuffing and then sew the top gap up by hand.

10 Complete the owl by hand sewing a small stitch to secure the top edge of each wing to the top of a stitching line on the front pocket.

cellphone pillow

Make a weighted pillow for your cellphone or tablet to rest its weary head! It will hold the screen at an ideal angle so you can read, or watch TV programs and movies while on a train or plane.

SKILL LEVEL

YOU WILL NEED

* 12 x 9 in. (30 x 22 cm) piece of green patterned fabric
* Green sewing thread
* Sewing machine
* 5½ x ¾ in. (14 x 2 cm) piece of thick card
* Fiberfill stuffing
* Sewing needle
* Rice

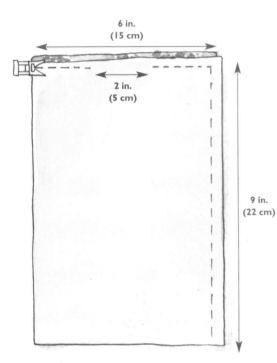

6 in. (15 cm)

2 in. (5 cm)

9 in. (22 cm)

1 Fold the fabric right sides together lengthwise so it measures 6 x 9 in. (15 x 22 cm). Sew for 2 in. (5 cm) along the top from the folded edge, leave a 2 in. (5 cm) gap, and then sew along the remaining top edge and down the side edge.

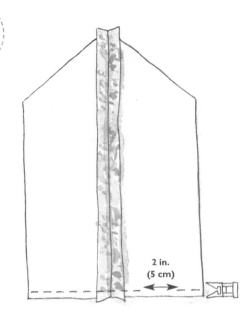

2 Fold the fabric so the side seam now runs down the center and sew across the short bottom seam, again leaving a 2 in. (5 cm) gap.

3 Turn the fabric inside out.

2 in.
(5 cm)

4 Thread the piece of card through the bottom hole and align so it is parallel to the seam, I in. (2.5 cm) up from the bottom edge. Sew around the edges of the card through all layers of fabric, using the sewing machine.

5 Fill the channel between the card and the bottom seam with stuffing to create a tightly packed ridge. Slipstitch to close the opening in the bottom seam.

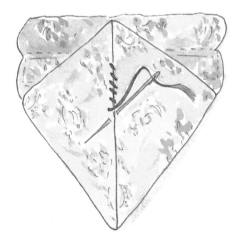

6 Fill the larger part of the pillow with a cup of rice from the top opening and then top up with more stuffing. Slipstitch the opening closed.

camera bag

Protect your valuable camera equipment with this spotty camera bag made from a favorite fabric, fleece, and foam.

SKILL LEVEL

YOU WILL NEED

* Spotty green fabric
* Cream fleece fabric
* Foam or yoga mat
* Sewing machine
* Needle and thread
* 5 pieces of hook-and-loop tape (Velcro) each 4 in. (10 cm) long
* 1 piece of hook-and-loop tape 10 in. (25 cm) long

1 Using the templates on pages 124–125, cut one template A, one template B, one template C, and two template D all from the green spotty fabric.

2 Cut two template A, two template B, two template C, one template E, and two template F all from the fleece fabric.

3 Cut three template G, four template H, one template I, and three template J all from the foam mat.

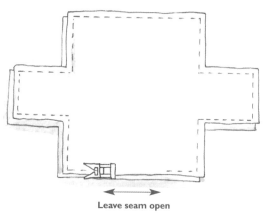

Leave seam open

4 Layer up the two fleece template A pieces wrong sides together and sew around the edges, leaving one long seam open.

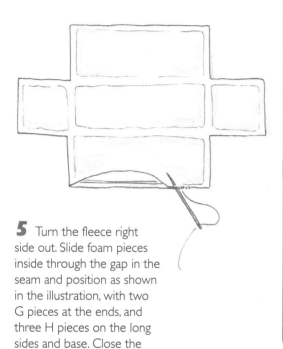

5 Turn the fleece right side out. Slide foam pieces inside through the gap in the seam and position as shown in the illustration, with two G pieces at the ends, and three H pieces on the long sides and base. Close the gap with slipstitch or overstitch (see page 114).

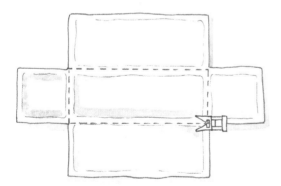

6 Using the sewing machine, sew between the foam pieces to secure them in position. Put this fleece piece to one side.

7 To make the handles, fold each template D strip of fabric in half right sides together and sew along the long seam. Turn right side out and press flat. Shape each handle as shown in the illustration.

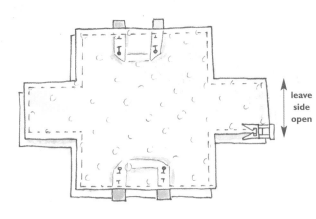

leave side open

8 Place the fabric template A piece right sides together onto the made-up fleece piece and insert a handle between the layers along each long seam, pointing inward as shown. Sew around the edges, leaving one short side open. Turn the piece right side out and close the gap with slipstitch or overstitch.

9 To make the lid of the bag, layer up the three template B pieces with one fleece piece right side up, the fabric piece right side down and the second fleece piece right side down on top of that. Sew around three sides, then turn so the fabric and one fleece piece are right side out. Insert the remaining template H piece of foam between the fleece layers and then sew up the hole with slipstitch or overstitch. Repeat to make the flap using the template C fabric and fleece pieces and the template I foam piece.

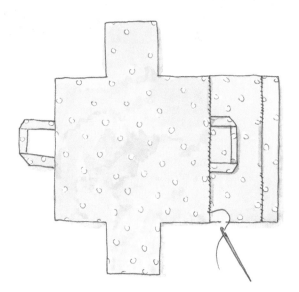

10 Slipstitch the larger lid piece to one long side of the bag. Slipstitch the smaller flap piece onto that, leaving a hole in this seam for the handle.

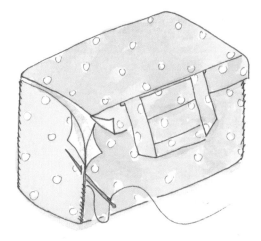

11 Sew up the corners of the bag using slipstitch.

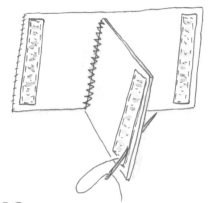

12 To make the dividers, fold fleece template E in half right sides together and sew along the side and bottom seam, leaving a gap for turning. Turn right side out, insert foam piece J and close the gap with slipstitch or overstitch. Fold one of the fleece template F pieces in half right sides together and sew along two of the seams. Turn right side out and insert two foam pieces J, then slipstitch or overstitch the gap closed. Sew the first foam piece to the center of the second at right angles using zigzag stitch. Sew the hook half of a short hook-and-loop strip to one side of each end as shown.

13 Make the other divider in the same way as in Step 12 but using just using fleece piece F and foam piece G. Sew the hook half of a short hook-and-loop strip to one side of each end.

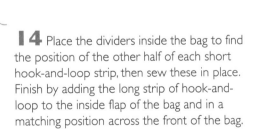

14 Place the dividers inside the bag to find the position of the other half of each short hook-and-loop strip, then sew these in place. Finish by adding the long strip of hook-and-loop to the inside flap of the bag and in a matching position across the front of the bag.

denim pocket phone tidy

Keep your phone, headphones, and charger together with this denim tidy made by upcycling a pair of old jeans.

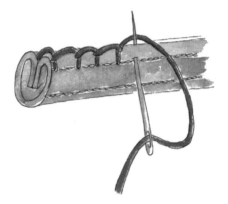

1 Start by making the handle. Cut out approximately 10 in. (20 cm) length of the inner leg seam of the jeans, leaving an extra $^1/_8$ in. (1 cm) of fabric on one side of the seam and $^3/_4$ in. (2 cm) on the other. Fold the narrower raw edge to the wrong side, then fold over the wider edge twice, so all the raw edges are inside as shown in the illustration. Blanket stitch down both edges in red floss (see page 115).

2 Cut out the complete mini coin pocket on the front of the jeans, leaving $^3/_8$ in. (1 cm) of extra fabric around the edge. Cut out a complete back pocket, leaving 1 in. (2.5 cm) of extra fabric all around the edge. Cut a piece of flower print fabric $^3/_8$ in. (1 cm) smaller than the front layer of the back pocket.

3 Iron Bondaweb onto the wrong side of a remaining scrap of the fabric and cut out three flowers from the design. Remove the paper backing and iron the flowers onto the front of the mini coin pocket. Work blanket stitch in orange floss along the top of the pocket. Add a French knot (see page 115) to the center of each flower using lime green embroidery floss.

4 Iron Bondaweb onto the wrong side of the fabric pocket shape. Remove the paper backing and iron the fabric to the center on the front of the back pocket. Secure by stitching around the edge in jade green floss. Iron a piece of Bondaweb onto the back of the complete mini coin pocket, remove the paper backing and then iron the mini pocket to the center of the flower print fabric shape, folding the raw edges underneath. Secure by working straight stitches in yellow embroidery floss.

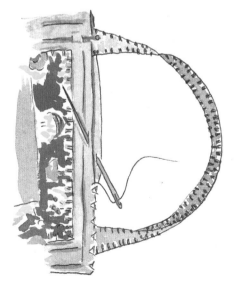

5 Cut a piece from the plain leg fabric of the jeans the same size as the complete back pocket piece. Place this right sides together with the back pocket piece and sew around the sides and base with a $^3/_8$ in. (1 cm) seam allowance. Turn right side out and insert the ends of the handle between the layers on the top edge. Sew the top edges together using slipstitch, securing the handle at the same time.

MP3 player exercise armband

Pump up the volume! Keep motivated during your workout with this jersey armband to hold your MP3 player.

SKILL LEVEL ✳ ✳ ✳

YOU WILL NEED

* 25 x 5½ in. (62.5 x 14 cm) of patterned jersey fabric
* Tape measure
* Scissors
* Sewing machine
* Thread to match fabric

1 Cut one piece of fabric 12 x 5½ in. (30 x 14 cm) and another 11 x 5½ in. (27.5 x 14 cm).

2 On the longer piece of fabric turn over both of the shorter ends to the wrong side by ³⁄₈ in. (1 cm) to make a hem and sew two lines of stitching down each.

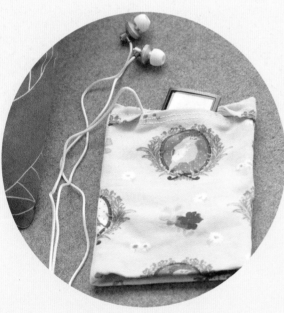

3 Fold over so that you create a ring, with one end overlapping the other by ¾ in. (2 cm). Overstitch the overlap in place on each side.

4 Fold the remaining piece of fabric in half with right sides together and sew across the short ends with a $3/8$ in. (1 cm) hem.

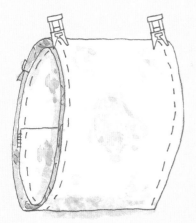

5 Slide this piece over the other, with right sides together, and sew around both edges.

6 Turn the armband right side out through the overlapping opening and adjust the fabric so the pocket opening is near the top edge and the armband is a neat ring. Slide your MP3 player into the pocket and you are ready to run!

USB beaded bracelet

Never lose your important files again with this ingenious bracelet that contains a USB stick hidden inside the fastening!

YOU WILL NEED

* ✱ 2 x 8 in. (5 x 20 cm) of silver foil jersey fabric
* ✱ Scissors
* ✱ Needle and thread
* ✱ USB stick with separate lid
* ✱ Superglue
* ✱ Fiberfill stuffing
* ✱ Assorted glass beads and bugle beads

1 Fold the strip of fabric in half lengthwise and sew along the long raw edges with a ¼ in. (3 mm) seam allowance. Turn right side out to make a ¾ × 8 in. (2 × 20 cm) tube.

2 Turn the raw edge of one short end into the tube and insert the USB stick all the way in so only the metal bit is left outside. Stick securely in place with a little dab of superglue.

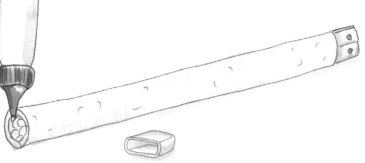

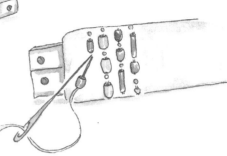

3 Fill the tube with stuffing, turn the raw fabric end in and secure with a dab of superglue. Then insert the USB stick lid into the tube end and secure with a dab of glue.

4 Decorate both ends of the bracelet by stitching an assortment of beads onto the flat areas of fabric over the USB stick and lid.

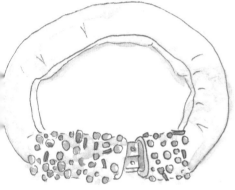

5 Close the two ends of the USB stick to complete the bracelet.

btw...

You may need to increase or reduce the length of the fabric strip at the start, depending on wrist size and the tightness of fit you want.

hair tool tidy

Never burn your carpet again! Make a clever hair tool tidy using only a plastic drainage pipe personalized with decoupage and sparkling rhinestone crystals.

1 Spray paint the drainage pipe in your chosen color. Allow to dry and then give it a second coat. Allow to dry completely.

2 Water down the PVA glue slightly and cut your decoupage paper into small squares. Apply the glue and then add paper squares to the top and bottom sections of the pipe in a striped design.

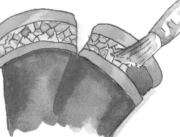

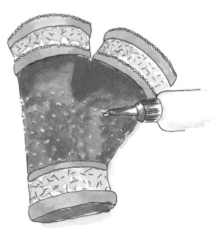

3 Using the superglue, apply scattered rhinestones to the body of the pipe and along the decoupaged sections. Allow to dry before using.

CHAPTER 3

PROTECT
YOUR TECH

Your gadgets cost a lot of money so you
need to protect them from the bumps
and scratches caused by everyday life.
There are a variety of ways to decorate
a phone case—cross stitch, resin,
rhinestones, and more. Try making
a case for your tablet, camera, or
e-reader using crochet or sewing.
The only limit is your imagination!

btw...

The fabric quantities are for a case to fit an iPad, so amend the dimensions following the instructions in step 1 if your tablet is smaller or larger.

felt tablet case

Personalize the icons on your particular brand of tablet to make a unique case, which will also keep it safe from scratches and bumps.

1 To make the outer case, measure your tablet and add 2½ in. (6 cm) onto the width to allow for the depth of the tablet and the seam allowances, and 3¼ in. (8 cm) onto the length to allow for the depth, seam allowances, and closing flap. Cut two pieces of gray felt this size and one piece of black felt 7¼ x 6 in. (18 x 15 cm) for the screen. Cut a piece of pale blue felt to 1¼ x 6 in. (3.5 x 15 cm).

SKILL LEVEL ✳ ✳ ✳

YOU WILL NEED
* ✳ 12 x 28 in. (30 x 70 cm) of gray felt (see step 1)
* ✳ 9 x 6 in. (19 x 15 cm) of black felt
* ✳ 2 x 6 in. (5 x 15 cm) of pale blue felt
* ✳ Tape measure
* ✳ Scissors
* ✳ Sewing needle and thread to match fabrics
* ✳ Embroidery floss in cream, black, gray, orange, yellow, green, aqua, blue, purple, violet, red, and dark brown
* ✳ Scraps of felt in green, cream, red, turquoise, yellow, coral, purple, brown, and mustard
* ✳ Sewing machine
* ✳ 2 snap fasteners

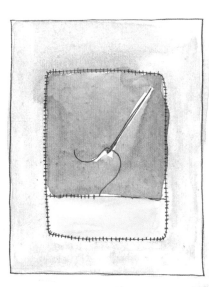

2 Using black thread and straight stitch, sew the black piece to one of the grey pieces, 1¾ in. (4.5 cm) up from the bottom and centered between each side to make the front screen. Stitch the strip of pale blue to the bottom of the black screen using blue thread and small straight stitches.

3 Use cream embroidery floss and a combination of backstitch and satin stitch to sew the reception, time, and battery life icons just below the top edge of the black screen. See pages 114–115 for how to work embroidery stitches.

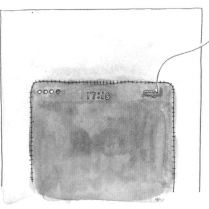

4 You can personalize the icons to your own style of tablet or use the ones I have designed. Each icon is ⁷⁄₈ in. (2 cm) square.

Text Message icon (A): cut a green square and a cream speech bubble. Stitch the speech bubble to the background using cream thread and tiny running stitches.

Calendar icon (B): cut a cream square and a narrow red strip. Sew the strip across the top of the square using red thread and tiny running stitches. Embroider the date in backstitch using black floss.

Camera icon (C): cut a grey square and a black camera. Sew the camera to the square using black thread. Embroider the detail using backstitch in gray floss.

Photos icon (D): cut a cream square and embroider segments of color using satin stitch and floss in orange, yellow, green, aqua, blue, purple, violet, and red.

Videos icon (E): cut a turquoise square and a cream strip. Sew the strip to the top of the square with cream thread. Embroider chevrons in satin stitch using black floss.

Maps icon (F): cut a green square and cream roads. Stitch the roads to the square with cream thread. Using floss, embroider a blue line using backstitch and a blue road sign using satin stitch. Add a red line in backstitch across the top of the road sign and a yellow road in satin stitch.

Reminders icon (G): cut a cream square. Make French knot dots on the left and running stitch lines using floss in four different colors.

Weather icon (H): cut a pale blue square and a cream cloud. Sew the cloud to the square using cream thread and then use yellow floss to sew a sun in satin stitch.

Games icon (I): cut a cream square and different size circles in turquoise, yellow, coral, and purple. Using matching thread, sew the circles to the square so they overlap.

Clock icon (J): cut a brown square and a cream circle. Sew the circle to the square using dark brown thread and straight stitch to indicate the hour positions. Sew the two hands of the clock using backstitch in brown floss. Sew a red line in backstitch for the second hand.

App Store icon (K): cut a turquoise square, then sew an A inside a circle using backstitch and cream floss.

Calculator icon (L): cut a mustard square and a smaller grey square. Sew the small square to the bottom right corner of the larger one. Using black floss sew plus, minus, multiplication, and equals symbols in the corners.

Passbook icon (M): cut a turquoise square, a green rectangle, and a mustard strip. Sew the green rectangle across the center of the turquoise square and add the mustard strip across the bottom. Use cream floss and satin stitch to add a detail to the left side of each strip.

Notes icon (N): cut a cream square and a mustard strip. Sew the strip across the top of the square. Embroider lines using brown floss and running stitch across the cream section.

YouTube icon (O): cut a red square and a smaller cream rectangle. Sew the rectangle to the center of the square and then use red floss and satin stitch to sew a triangle in the center of the cream rectangle.

FaceTime icon (P): cut a green square and a cream camera. Sew the camera to the square with cream thread. Embroider lines in backstitch with green floss for the detail on the camera.

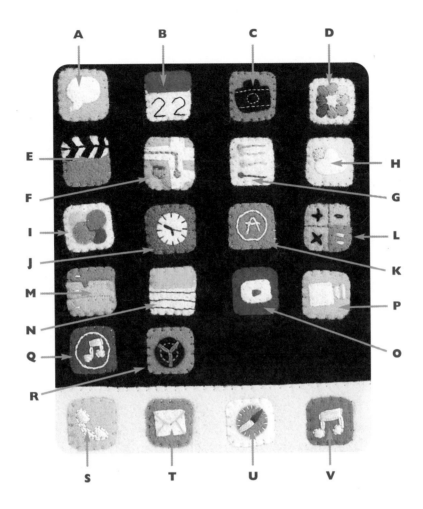

Music Store icon (Q): cut a purple square and embroider a music symbol inside a circle using backstitch and satin stitch in cream floss.

Settings icon (R): cut a grey square and a black circle. Sew the circle to the square with a circle of backstitch using gray thread. Add the three arms in backstitch in gray floss.

Phone icon (S): cut a green square and embroider a phone shape using satin stitch in cream floss.

Mail icon (T): cut a turquoise square and a cream rectangle. Sew the rectangle to the square using cream thread. Add the lines for the envelope detail using backstitch in turquoise floss.

Internet icon (U): cut a cream square and turquoise circle. Sew the circle to the square using cream thread. Embroider lines out from the center in red and cream floss, using satin stitch.

Music icon (V): cut a coral square and embroider a music symbol using satin stitch in cream floss.

5 Sew all the icons onto the screen with straight stitch in a matching color thread, using the photograph as a guide for position.

6 Cut a black felt circle for the home button and sew below the screen in the center using straight stitch in black thread. Add a long oval strip of black felt over the top of the screen for the receiver, stitching it in place using running stitch in gray embroidery floss. Sew two French knots in black floss for cameras on the left and above the receiver strip.

7 Trim 1³/₈ in. (3.5cm) off one short end of the gray felt piece for the back. Place the back and front pieces right sides together and sew around the sides and bottom with a sewing machine, taking a ⁵/₈ in. (1.5cm) seam allowance.

8 Turn the case right side out and then shape the extra piece at the top of the front piece into a flap. Sew the two snap fasteners to the underside of the flap and in a matching position on the back of the case, as closures.

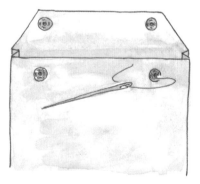

cup of tea
e-reader case

What's better than being curled
up on a cold evening with a
good read and a nice cup of
tea? Make your e-reader a
cozy felt case in the shape
of a mug of tea to remind
you of those times.

fyi...

Check the size of
the template before
cutting and tweak
it slightly to fit your
brand of e-reader
if necessary.

SKILL LEVEL

YOU WILL NEED

* 12 x 40 in. (30 x 100cm) of
  ³/₁₆ in. (4 mm) thick pink felt
* 16 in. (40 cm) of 2 in. (5 cm)
  wide elastic
* Scissors
* Sewing machine and pink
  thread

* 2 x 4 in. (5 x 10 cm) of ¹/₁₆ in.
  (1 mm) thick cream felt
* Stranded cotton embroidery
  floss in pink, turquoise, and
  mustard
* Needle
* 12 in. (30 cm) of string

* 15 in. (37.5 cm) of turquoise
  lace trim
* 15 in. (37.5 cm) of mustard
  mini ric rac

1 Using the templates on page
126, cut out the double mug
template and mug window
template from the thick pink felt.
Cut the elastic into four equal
pieces and pin a strip across
each corner on the wrong
side of the window. Put the
window piece on top of the
right-hand half of the double mug,
with both pieces right side up, and
sew around the edges with the
sewing machine using pink thread.

2 Trim the elastic close to the outer stitching so the edges are not sticking out.

3 Using the tea bag template, cut out two pieces from the cream felt. Embroider a heart in satin stitch using turquoise floss in the center of one tea bag shape. Work running stitch around the heart using pink floss.

4 Sew the end of the string to the back of the heart on the tea bag. Add the second tea bag shape as a backing and then sew the two pieces together all around the edge using blanket stitch in mustard floss.

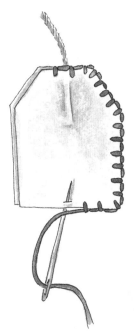

5 Fold the double mug shape in half with the window on the inside, and trap the other end of the tea bag string down the top of the fold. Sew down the spine close to the edge of the mug using the sewing machine, holding the string in place at the same time.

6 Decorate the front by sewing a length of turquoise lace to the top and bottom edges and lengths of ric rac 1 in. (2.5 cm) away from the edges of the lace, using the sewing machine. Secure the top of the teabag in place by hand to complete.

cross stitch phone case

YOU WILL NEED

* Pre-punched cellphone case
* Stranded cotton embroidery floss in dark blue, turquoise, mustard, lemon yellow, dark red, coral, purple, lilac, dark green, lime green, orange, peach, cream, and gray
* Needle
* Scissors

If factory-made cellphone cases don't do it for you, get stitching on a pre-punched case. Cross stitch and running stitch are used in this design but you can let your imagination run wild! If you can't find a pre-punched case for your model, try punching holes with a sharp needle into a silicon case.

1 Decide on your design—you can either use the design on page 126, or work up your own design on a piece of squared paper. If you use the design provided, you may have to adjust it to suit your case.

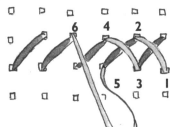

2 Using the first color, divide the stranded cotton floss into two sets of three strands. Thread one set of strands into the needle and tie a knot in the end.

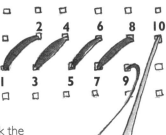

3 Work the bottom leg of all the cross stitches from bottom left to top right first. The bottom stitches of my crosses are worked in the darker set of colors: dark blue, mustard, dark red, purple, dark green, and orange.

4 The top stitches that go from bottom right to top left are worked in the lighter colors: turquoise, lemon yellow, coral, lilac, lime green, and peach.

5 Fill the spaces between the triangles with cream cross stitches, working both legs in the same color.

6 To complete your case, work gray running stitches (see page 114) in between each triangle.

btw...

To make your own design, draw out the size of your phone case on a piece of squared paper, with each square representing one stitch.

YOU WILL NEED

* Silicon cellphone case
* Pen
* Craft knife and cutting mat
* 6 x 3 in. (15 x 7.5 cm) piece of thin pink cardstock
* Scrap of gold cardstock
* PVA glue

laser cut phone case

Flower power! Silicon cellphone covers are really easy to cut into and then back with colored card to create a cool laser-cut effect.

1 Place the cellphone case outer side down onto the main template on page 126 and trace the design onto the inside surface using a pen.

2 Using a sharp craft knife, carefully cut out the shapes in the design.

3 Using the template, cut out a piece of pink cardstock to fit inside the bottom of the case. Cut out the shape for the camera lens.

fyi...

You may need to insert the pink piece into the cellphone case to check the positioning of the gold flowers is correct, before sticking the flowers down.

4 From the gold cardstock, cut the two flowers. Stick the gold flowers onto the pink cardstock under the corresponding cut-out flowers.

5 Allow to dry before assembling and placing your cellphone in the case.

vintage book e-reader case

Disguise the fact you are using an e-reader by popping it into this case made from an old book that has been hollowed out!

SKILL LEVEL

YOU WILL NEED

* **Vintage book larger than your e-reader**
* **Ruler**
* **Pencil**
* **Paintbrush**
* **PVA glue**
* **Craft knife**

1 Measure your e-reader and add an extra ³/₈ in. (1 cm) to the length and width.

2 Cut out a page of the book that you find attractive and put to one side—this will become the page that neatens the base of the recess that holds the e-reader. If you want, you can choose another page from the book to stick on top of the first page—this will become the border around the recess, so choose a page with text or illustrations close to the edge of the page.

3 Mix up a solution of 70% glue and 30% water and, using a paintbrush, paint the outside edges of the pages, holding the front book cover up so it doesn't get stuck too. Allow to dry.

4 Once dry, mark out the e-reader size in the center of the top page and then cut out using the craft knife. You do not need to go the full depth of the book, just as deep as the e-reader plus a little extra.

5 Paint the inside edges of the book and the base page with the same 70/30% glue and water mix. Allow to dry.

6 To complete the book, mark out the e-reader shape on the page you selected in step 2 in the same place as the other pages and cut out. Stick the cut-out piece to the base of the recess to cover any glue spots—do not cover this one with glue, keep it dry and clean. Repeat for the border around the recess. Allow to dry before using.

crochet camera case

Crochet a vintage camera for a stylish case as cool as the photographs you take! And you only need to master a few simple crochet stitches.

SKILL LEVEL

YOU WILL NEED

* I oz (25 g) of light worsted (DK) cotton yarn in teal
* I oz (25 g) of light worsted (DK) cotton yarn in cream
* I oz (25 g) of light worsted (DK) cotton yarn in gray
* ⅜ oz (10 g) of light worsted (DK) cotton yarn in mustard
* US size C2/D3 (3 mm) crochet hook
* Pins
* Felt scraps in pink, green, white, and black
* Black and cream embroidery floss
* Yarn needle
* 4 in. (10 cm) cream zipper
* Sewing machine or sewing needle and cream thread

GAUGE (TENSION)

* 24 stitches x 26 rows over a 4-in. (10-cm) square using a US size C2/D3 (3 mm) crochet hook

FINISHED SIZE

* This case is 4½ x 4¼ in. (11.5 x 11 cm), but see Step 1 for how to adjust the size for your own camera

1 Measure your camera. Using the teal yarn make a length of chain stitch 2 in. (5 cm) longer than your camera is wide, adding I chain stitch for turning. For this case it was 27 chain stitches plus I for turning.

Row 1: Insert the crochet hook into the second stitch of the chain and work a single crochet stitch; repeat in every stitch along the row so you have 27 stitches. Chain 1 and turn.

Row 2: Insert the crochet hook into the first single crochet stitch and work I single crochet; repeat in every stitch along the row so you have 27 stitches. Chain 1 and turn.

2 Repeat Row 2 until your piece is as long as the height of your camera plus 2 in. (5 cm). For my camera this was 25 rows. Cut your yarn and thread through the loop to secure.

CROCHET TERMINOLOGY

US and UK crochet patterns share stitch names but these do not refer to the same stitches.

This crochet pattern is written using US crochet terminology. See pages 118–120 for details of how to work each stitch. In this pattern, please note that:

Single crochet (US) = **double crochet** (UK)

Half-double crochet (US) = **half-treble crochet** (UK)

3 Change to cream yarn and make another chain of 28 stitches. Work a third of the number of rows that you did for the teal section—so for my camera I worked 8 rows. Repeat steps 1–3 to make the back of the case.

4 To make the lens piece, using the gray yarn, make a chain of 3 stitches and then join into a circle with a slip stitch.

Round 1: Chain 1, work 5 single crochet into the circle, join to the first stitch with a slip stitch.

Round 2: Chain 1, work 2 single crochet into each stitch (so there are 10 stitches), join to the first stitch with a slip stitch.

Round 3: Chain 1, *work 1 single crochet into the next stitch, then work 2 single crochet into the following stitch; repeat from * to the end. Join to the first stitch with a slip stitch. (15 stitches)

Round 4: Chain 1, *work 1 single crochet into each of the next 2 stitches, then work 2 single crochet into the following stitch; repeat from * to the end. Join to the first stitch with a slip stitch. (20 stitches)

Round 5: Chain 1, *work 1 single crochet into each of the next 3 stitches, then work 2 single crochet into the following stitch; repeat from * to the end. Join to the first stitch with a slip stitch. (25 stitches)

5 Change to cream yarn.
Round 6: Chain 2, *work 1 half-double crochet into each of next 4 stitches, then work 2 half-double crochet into next stitch; repeat from * to the end. Join to the first stitch with a slip stitch. (30 stitches) Cut the yarn and thread through the loop to secure.

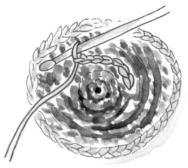

6 To make the reflection on the lens, either sew a line of chain stitch (see page 115) using cream yarn and a yarn needle or use your crochet hook to make 7 surface crochet stitches (see page 120).

7 Sew in all the loose ends. Block the pieces by pinning them to an ironing board and gently steam ironing.

8 With both pieces right side up, pin one cream piece so it is just overlapping the top edge of a teal piece and, using your crochet hook, surface crochet the pieces together using mustard yarn. Repeat with the other cream and teal pieces.

9 Pin the lens onto the front of the camera and, using your crochet hook, surface crochet the lens in place using gray yarn.

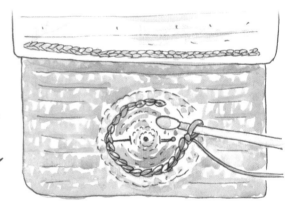

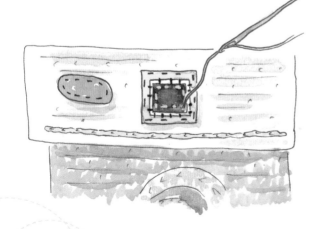

10 Cut an oval from the pink felt and rectangles in descending size from the black, cream, and green felt. Use embroidery floss and running stitch to attach them to the cream strip on the front of the camera, following the photograph for positioning.

11 Make the strap by making a chain of 4 stitches using gray yarn and then working rows of 3 single crochet stitches until the strap is the desired length (approximately 8 in./20 cm).

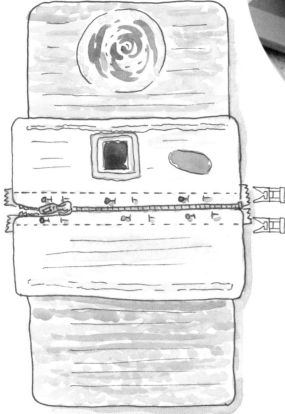

12 With both the zipper and the crochet pieces right side up, pin the top edges of the two cream pieces along the zipper tape on either side as shown. Using a sewing machine or hand stitching, sew the zipper in place.

13 Insert the ends of the folded-over strap between the front and back pieces in the center of the cream section and pin in place. Work single crochet around the edge to join the sides together, using cream around the top and teal around the base.

popsicle phone case

**This cute and smart little case will let your cellphone
sit snugly inside a sweet and colorful popsicle.**

SKILL LEVEL ✳ ✳ ✳

YOU WILL NEED

* ✳ 4 x 6 in. (10 x 15 cm) of red
  pattern fabric
* ✳ 4 x 8 in. (10 x 20 cm) of pink
  pattern fabric
* ✳ 4 x 18 in. (10 x 45 cm) of
  orange pattern fabric
* ✳ 2 x 6 in. (5 x 15 cm) of
  striped fabric

* ✳ Pins
* ✳ Fabric scissors
* ✳ Felt
* ✳ Tape measure or ruler
* ✳ Needle and thread to
  match fabrics
* ✳ Iron

* ✳ Green embroidery floss
* ✳ Split ring
* ✳ Snap fastener
* ✳ Sewing machine (optional)

1 Using the templates on page 127, cut two top
pieces in red fabric, two middle pieces in pink, and
two bottom pieces in orange. Cut two of the
whole piece in orange and in the felt. Cut a stick
piece from the striped fabric. Cut two side pieces
from each of the pink and orange fabrics.

2 To make the popsicle
outer, place a top piece
right sides together to a
middle piece, aligning the
long straight edge. Sew by
hand or on a machine
with a ¼ in. (5 mm) seam
allowance. Add a bottom
piece on the other side of
the middle piece in the
same way. Repeat with the
other three pieces and
press all the seams open.

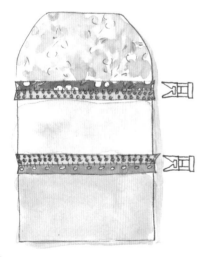

3 Lay one outer piece right side
up onto a piece of felt, with raw
edges aligned. Sew the running
stitch design of the popsicle
through both layers in green floss,
using the photograph and drawing
as a guide. Repeat with the other
outer and felt piece.

fyi...

To adapt the pattern to your cellphone, place it on the pattern before cutting and make sure that there is an extra $5/8$ in. (1.5 cm) all round for seams.

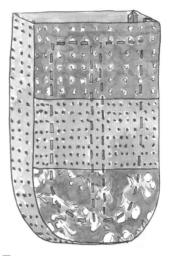

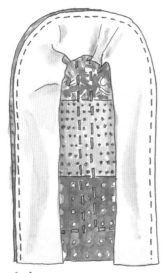

4 With right sides together, pin and then sew the pink fabric side piece around the sides and top edge of one of the outer pieces.

5 Sew the other outer piece to the other edge of the side piece to create a little pocket. Turn right side out and put to one side.

6 To make the lining, repeat steps 4 and 5 with the popsicle and side pieces in the orange fabric, but do not turn right side out.

7 To make the popsicle stick, fold all the raw edges of the stick piece over to the wrong side by ¼ in. (5 mm) and press flat.

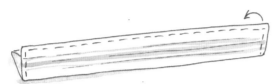

8 Fold the popsicle stick in half lengthwise and press flat. Sew around the three open edges.

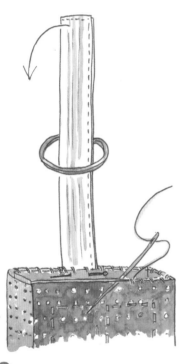

10 Stitch the two halves of the snap fastener to opposite sides of the inside of the stick, near the base of the popsicle. Sew a line of running stitch across the stick just below the split ring to complete.

9 Push the lining inside the outer. Turn in the raw edges and then insert one end of the stick between the layers in the middle of one long edge and pin in place. Thread the split ring onto the stick, then insert the other end between the layers on the other side. Slipstitch the folded edges of the layers together all around, securing the ends of the stick at the same time.

oilcloth iPad stand

Ideal for use in the kitchen when you are cooking, this oilcloth stand is wipe clean and holds your tablet in a standing position for easy viewing.

1 Cut the MDF board into the following sizes and number each one.

Piece 1 – 9½ × 7 in. (24 × 17.5 cm)
Piece 2 – 9½ × ½ in. (24 × 1.2 cm)
Piece 3 – 9½ × 7½ in. (24 × 19 cm)
Piece 4 – 9½ × ½ in. (24 × 1.2 cm)
Piece 5 – 9½ × 3½ in. (24 × 9 cm)

2 Cut the fabric into the following pieces:

Piece 1 – 10½ × 23 in. (26.5 × 57.5 cm)
Piece 2 – 10½ × 15½ in. (26.5 × 39 cm)
Piece 3 – 10½ × 8 in. (26.5 × 20 cm)

3 Take fabric piece 3 and place a short piece of elastic across each corner. Sew in place at each edge of the fabric using the sewing machine. Trim off the protruding ends of elastic.

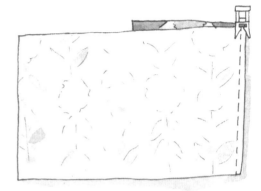

4 Place fabric piece 2 right sides together with fabric piece 3 and sew together along one edge. Press the seam open and open out flat.

5 Place fabric piece 1 right side together on top of the joined pieces. Sew together at the short end with the elastic pieces. Mark 2 in. (5 cm) from the stitch line and then pin the long piece of elastic in the center of this line between the layers.

6 Sew along both long sides to make a big pocket and then turn right side out through the open end.

7 Insert board piece 1 right down into the pocket to the end. Sew along the first seam between fabric pieces 3 and 2, using the sewing machine.

8 Repeat with the remaining four pieces of board in order, stitching down as close as possible to each one before adding the next. Tuck in the remaining fabric at the end and close the opening with an overstitch.

rhinestone phone case

Shine bright like a diamond by encrusting your phone cover with an assortment of gems for a glamorous effect.

SKILL LEVEL ✱✱✱

YOU WILL NEED

* Cellphone cover for your model
* Cardstock
* Pencil
* Scissors
* Assorted rhinestones in emerald green, aqua, clear, gold, orange, and rose gold
* Superglue
* Tweezers
* Varnish

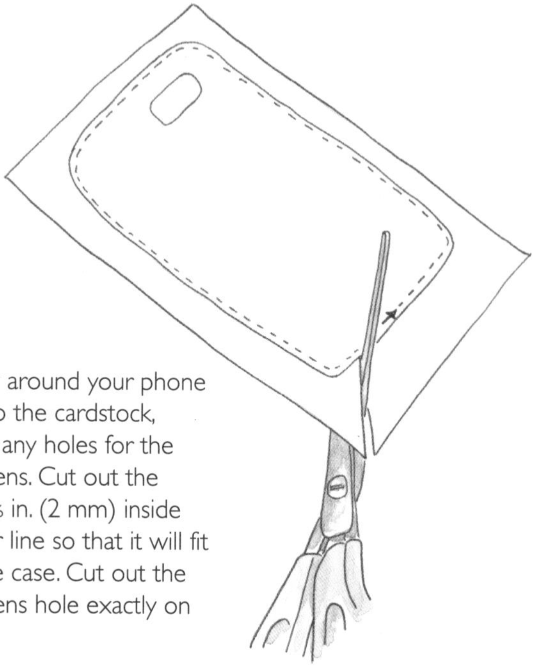

1 Draw around your phone case onto the cardstock, including any holes for the camera lens. Cut out the shape 1/16 in. (2 mm) inside the outer line so that it will fit inside the case. Cut out the camera lens hole exactly on the line.

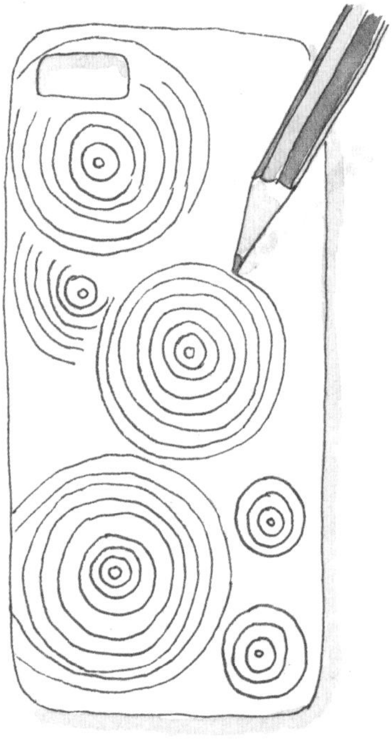

2 Draw your pattern on the cardstock insert—this does not need to be precise, just a rough layout. I have created a circles design.

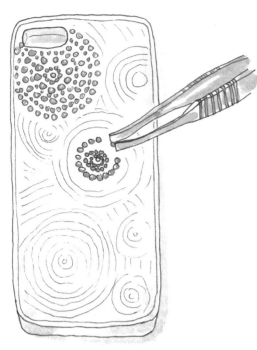

3 Place the cardstock insert into the phone case and then begin sticking the gems to the outside of the case. Apply a small area of glue only and add the gems using a pair of tweezers. Work small sections at a time as the glue dries very quickly.

4 Once the design is complete and dry, add a layer of varnish to seal the phone case and hide any white residue from the superglue.

pressed flower resin phone case

Dry flowers from the garden or from a special bouquet and keep them forever by preserving them in resin.

 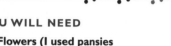
YOU WILL NEED

* Flowers (I used pansies and gypsophila)
* Absorbent paper
* Heavy books or flower press
* Cellphone cover for your model
* Superglue
* Resin casting chemicals
* Disposable container
* Iridescent glitter
* Popsicle stick
* Cotton bud

1 Space your flowers apart between two sheets of absorbent paper and place under a pile of heavy books or into a flower press. Place in a warm dry place (a linen closet is ideal) and allow to dry for up to three weeks or until they are completely dry.

2 Arrange your flowers on the phone case and then stick in place using dabs of superglue. Allow to dry.

3 Mix the resin according to the instructions—I used 4 fl oz (100 ml) resin with ½ teaspoon (2 ml) of hardener. Add about a teaspoon of glitter and mix well.

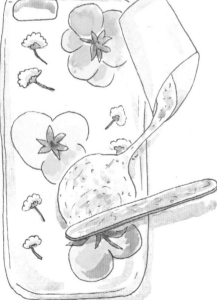

4 Very slowly pour the resin onto the surface of the phone case and use the popsicle stick to gradually push it to the edges. Ensure none goes over the edge of the phone case—if it does, clean away with a cotton bud.

5 Allow to dry completely before using. This should take approximately 48 hours, depending on your resin.

btw...

It can take up to three weeks for the pressed flowers to dry out completely so allow plenty of time if you are making this for a gift.

sewing techniques

RUNNING AND STRAIGHT STITCH

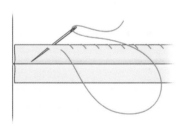

This is a long, straight stitch. Large running stitches can be used for basting (tacking). Straight stitches are running stitches worked parallel to each other rather than end to end.

BACK STITCH

1 Bring the thread up through the fabric and work a stitch backward, coming up a stitch length in front of the last stitch.

2 Work the next stitch from the end of the first stitch, again coming up a stitch length in front. Repeat to the end. This gives the effect of a continuous line.

OVERSTITCH

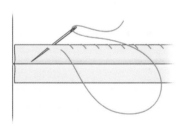

Also known as oversewing, this stitch is used to close openings, but also to neaten edges. Either bring two folded edges together or work along one raw edge. Bring the needle out from back to front, over the edge, and out from back to front again, a bit further along. Work along the edge in this way making diagonal stitches, which draws the two sides together if closing an opening.

SLIPSTITCH

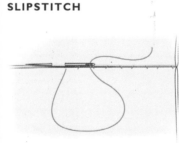

This is used to join folded edges. Working from right to left, bring the needle through one folded edge, slip the needle through the fold of the opposite edge for about ¼ in. (5 mm) and draw the thread through.

SATIN STITCH

This is used to fill in a shape. Work straight stitches to the outline of the shape and keeping the edges even. You may prefer to draw the shape onto the fabric first; if so, make sure that your stitches are worked to the outside of the marked line so it does not show.

CHAIN STITCH

This is used to create a decorative line. Bring the needle up through the fabric, back down next to where it came out and up a stitch length away. Loop the thread around the tip of the needle and pull through. Insert the needle inside the loop to begin the next stitch. At the end, make a small stitch over the last loop to secure.

BLANKET STITCH

1 Bring the thread out at the edge of the fabric at the top of the stitch. Take a vertical stitch through the fabric a short distance away and then loop the thread around the tip of the needle and pull it through.

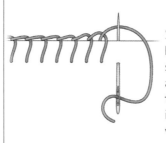

2 Take the next stitch the same way, keeping the vertical stitches all the same length and the same distance apart. At the end, take the needle to the reverse over the last loop to hold it in place, and fasten off on the reverse with two small stitches.

SEWING A SNAP FASTENER

Sew four hand stitches through each hole, without stitching right through to the other side of the fabric. Finish with a couple of small stitches under the snap to secure the thread end.

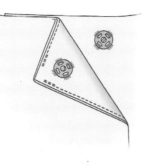

USING BONDAWEB

Bondaweb is fusible webbing on a backing paper and is a quick and easy way to attach layers of fabric together, keeping your design flat and ready for further decorative stitching. Iron a piece of Bondaweb rough side down onto the wrong side of the fabric to be applied. Peel off the paper backing and position the piece onto the right side of the base fabric. Iron in place.

FRENCH KNOT

1 Bring the needle up from the back of the fabric. Wrap the thread once or twice around the needle tip, then push the needle into the fabric right next to where it came up.

2 As you push the needle through, hold the wrapped threads tight against the fabric with a thumbnail. Pull the needle all the way through so the wraps form a small knot on the surface.

knitting techniques

SLIP KNOT

1 Lay the yarn end on the palm of your left hand, take it right round the top two fingers and down. Take the knitting needle over the upper strand from right to left; pick up the lower strand, as shown in the diagram. Pull the strand through to form a loop.

2 Slip the yarn off your fingers leaving the loop on the needle. Gently pull on both yarn ends to tighten the knot. Then pull on the yarn leading to the ball of yarn to tighten the knot on the needle.

CABLE CAST ON

1 Put the needle with the slip knot into your left hand. Insert the point of the other needle into the front of the slip knot and under the left needle. Wind the yarn from the ball of yarn around the tip of the right needle.

2 Using the tip of the needle, draw the yarn through the slip knot to form a loop, which is a new stitch. Slip the loop from the right needle onto the left needle.

3 For the next stitch, insert the tip of the right needle between the two stitches. Wind the yarn over the right needle, from left to right, then draw through to form a loop. Transfer this loop to the left needle. Repeat until you have cast on the right number of stitches for your project.

KNIT STITCH

1 Hold the needle with the cast-on stitches in your left hand, then insert the point of the right needle into the front of the first stitch from left to right. Wind the yarn around the point of the right needle, from left to right.

2 With the tip of the right needle, pull the yarn through the stitch to form a loop. This loop is your new stitch.

3 Slip the original stitch off the left needle by gently pulling the right needle to the right. Repeat the steps until you have knitted all the stitches on the left needle. To work the next row, transfer the needle with the stitches into your left hand.

PURL STITCH

1 Hold the needle with the stitches in your left hand, and then insert the point of the right needle into the front of the first stitch from right to left. Wind the yarn around the point of the right needle, from right to left.

2 With the tip of the right needle, pull the yarn through the stitch to form a loop. This loop is your new stitch.

3 Slip the original stitch off the left needle by gently pulling your right needle to the right. Repeat these steps till you have purled all the stitches on your left needle. To work the next row, transfer the needle with all the stitches into your left hand.

BINDING (CASTING) OFF

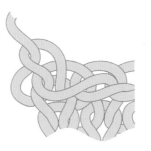

1 Knit two stitches in the normal way. With the point of the left needle, pick up the first stitch just knitted and lift it over the second stitch. Knit another stitch and repeat the process of lifting the first stitch over the second until there is just one stitch on the right needle.

2 Break the yarn, leaving a tail of yarn long enough to stitch your work together. Pull the tail through the last stitch.

KNIT 2 STITCHES TOGETHER

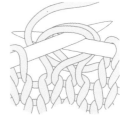

This is the simplest way of decreasing. Insert the needle through two stitches instead of one and then knit them in the normal way. Purl 2 stitches together in the same way, but working a purl stitch.

KNIT IN FRONT AND BACK

Start knitting your stitch in the normal way but instead of slipping the "old" stitch off the needle, knit into the back of it and then slip the "old" stitch off the needle in the normal way.

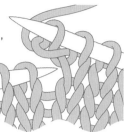

SLIP 1 STITCH, KNIT 1 STITCH, PASS SLIPPED STITCH OVER

Slip the first stitch from the left needle to the right, knit the next stitch, use the tip of the left needle to pass the slipped stitch over.

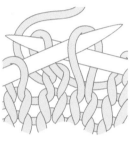

MAKE 1

Pick up the horizontal strand between the stitches on the needles. You can pick it up from front to back (as shown here, make 1 left) and knit into the back of the loop, or from back to front (which would be make 1 right) and knit into the front of the loop. Both methods twist the yarn to prevent a hole.

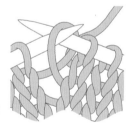

crochet techniques

CHAIN STITCH

1 Make a slip knot (see page 116) on the crochet hook. Holding the loop on the hook, yarn over hook from back to front, then catch the yarn in the hook.

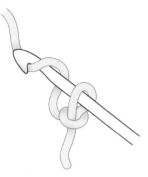

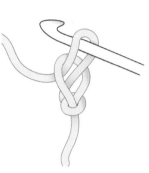

2 Pull the yarn through the loop on the crochet hook to make the second link in the chain. Continue in this way till the chain is the length that you need for your project.

SLIP STITCH

1 Insert the hook through the stitch (chain or chain space), yarn over hook.

2 Pull the yarn through both the stitch (chain or chain space) and the loop on the hook at the same time, so you will be left with one loop on the hook.

SINGLE CROCHET (US)

This stitch is known as double crochet in the UK.

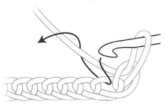 

I Insert the hook into the work, yarn over hook, pull the yarn through the work (two loops on hook).

2 Yarn over hook, pull through two loops on the hook. You will then have one loop on the hook.

MAKING A RING

I To join the chain into a circle, insert the crochet hook into the first chain you made (not into the slip knot), yarn over hook, then pull the yarn through the chain and through the loop on your hook at the same time, thereby creating a slip stitch and forming a circle.

HALF-DOUBLE CROCHET (US)

This stitch is known as half-treble crochet in the UK.

I Before inserting the hook into the work, wrap the yarn over, put the hook through the work with the yarn wrapped over.

2 Yarn over hook, pull through the first loop on the hook (three loops on hook).

3 Yarn over hook, pull the yarn through all three loops. You will then have one loop on the hook.

DOUBLE CROCHET (US)

This stitch is known as treble in the UK.

I Before inserting the hook into the work wrap the yarn over, put the hook through the work with the yarn wrapped over.

2 Yarn over hook again and pull through the first loop on the hook (three loops on hook). Yarn over hook again, pull the yarn through two loops (two loops on hook).

3 Pull the yarn through two loops again. You will then have one loop on the hook.

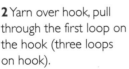

TREBLE (US)

This stitch is known as double treble crochet in the UK.

Yarn over hook twice, insert hook into the stitch, yarn over hook, pull a loop through (four loops on hook), yarn over hook, pull the yarn through two stitches (three loops on hook), yarn over hook, pull a loop through the next two stitches (two loops on hook), yarn over hook, pull a loop through the last two stitches.

SINGLE CROCHET 2 STITCHES TOGETHER (US)

This stitch is double crochet 2 stitches together in the UK.

1 Insert the hook into the work, yarn over hook and pull through (two loops on hook), insert the hook in the next stitch, yarn over hook and pull the yarn through.

2 Yarn over hook again and pull through all three loops on the hook. You will then have one loop on the hook.

HALF-DOUBLE CROCHET 2 STITCHES TOGETHER (US)

This stitch is half-treble crochet 2 stitches together in the UK. The basic technique for this is similar to single crochet 2 stitches together.

1 Yarn over hook, insert hook into next stitch, yarn over hook, draw yarn through. You now have three loops on the hook.

2 Yarn over hook, insert hook into next stitch, yarn over hook, draw yarn through. There are now five loops on the hook.

3 Yarn over hook and draw the yarn through all five loops on the hook. You will then have one loop on the hook.

SURFACE CROCHET

This creates a chain stitch on the surface, which can be used as decoration or to join overlapping pieces. The yarn is fed through from the back of the work.

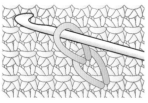

1 Create a slip knot and pull it through from the back to the front of the work using the crochet hook, at the point where you want the surface crochet to begin. Insert the hook into the work a stitch length away. On the back of the work, take the yarn over the hook once.

2 Pull the yarn through to the front of the work (two loops on hook). Pull the loop closest to the tip of the hook through the other to make a stitch. You will then have one loop on the hook.

3 Repeat to make more stitches. At the end, take the hook out of the last loop, insert it into the work from the back and pull the last loop through to the back. Yarn over hook and pull through the loop. Cut the yarn and darn in the ends.

templates

Here are all the templates you'll need for the projects in this book. Actual-size templates can be traced off the page. Half-size and quarter-size templates have been reduced to fit on the page and will need to be enlarged on a photocopier by the given percentage.

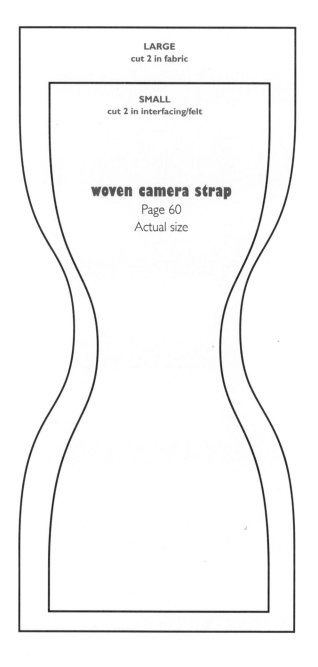

LARGE
cut 2 in fabric

SMALL
cut 2 in interfacing/felt

woven camera strap
Page 60
Actual size

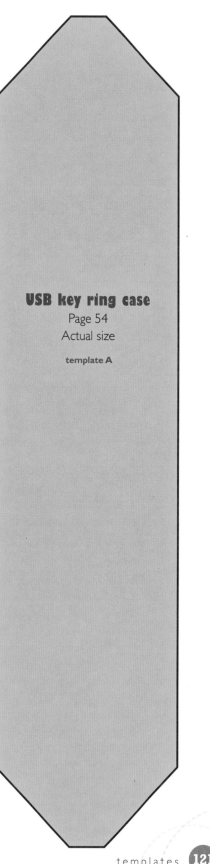

USB key ring case
Page 54
Actual size

template A

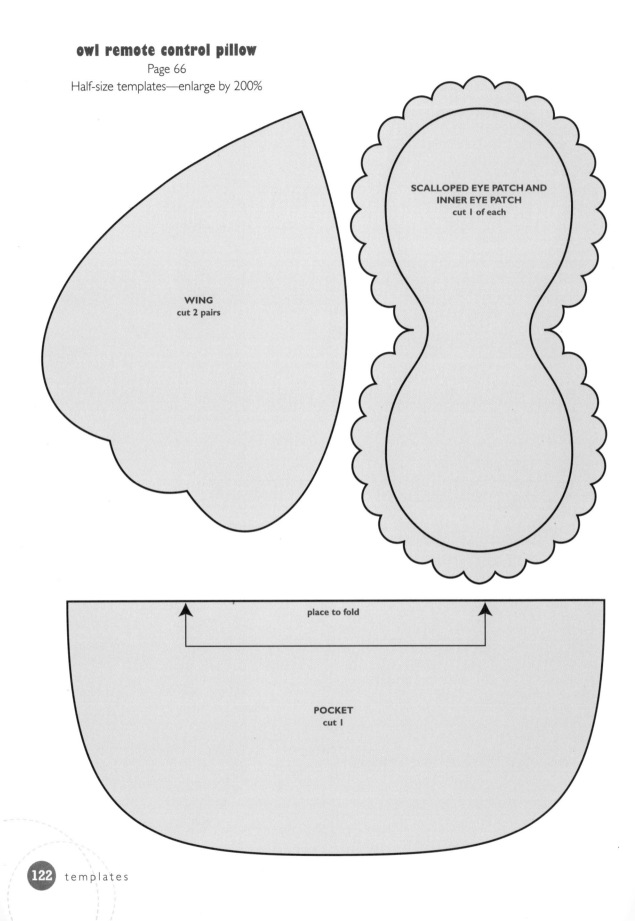

WING
cut 2 pairs

**SCALLOPED EYE PATCH AND
INNER EYE PATCH**
cut 1 of each

place to fold

POCKET
cut 1

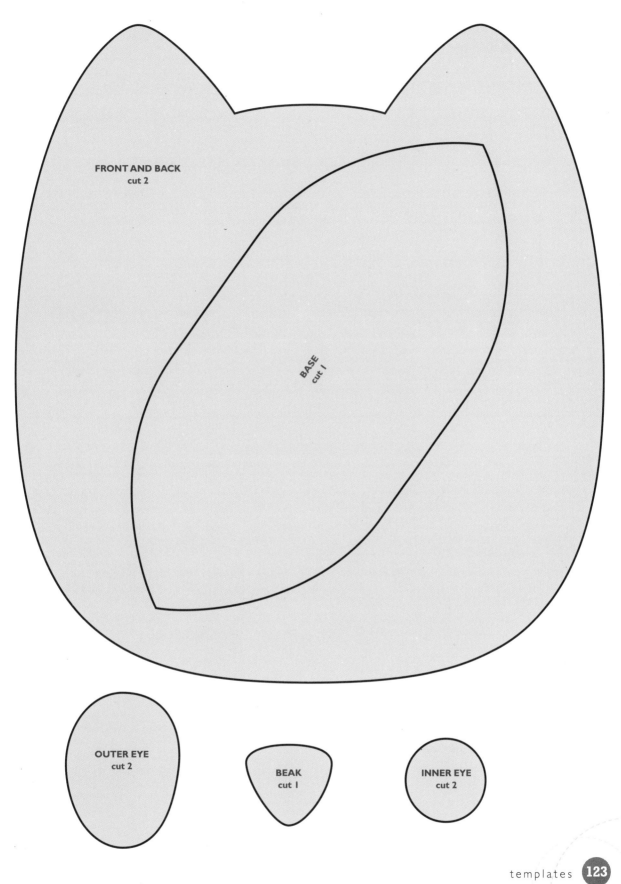

FRONT AND BACK
cut 2

BASE
cut 1

OUTER EYE
cut 2

BEAK
cut 1

INNER EYE
cut 2

camera bag

Page 72

These are quarter-size templates (so enlarge them by 400%), but you may find it easier simply to draw them to the dimensions shown.

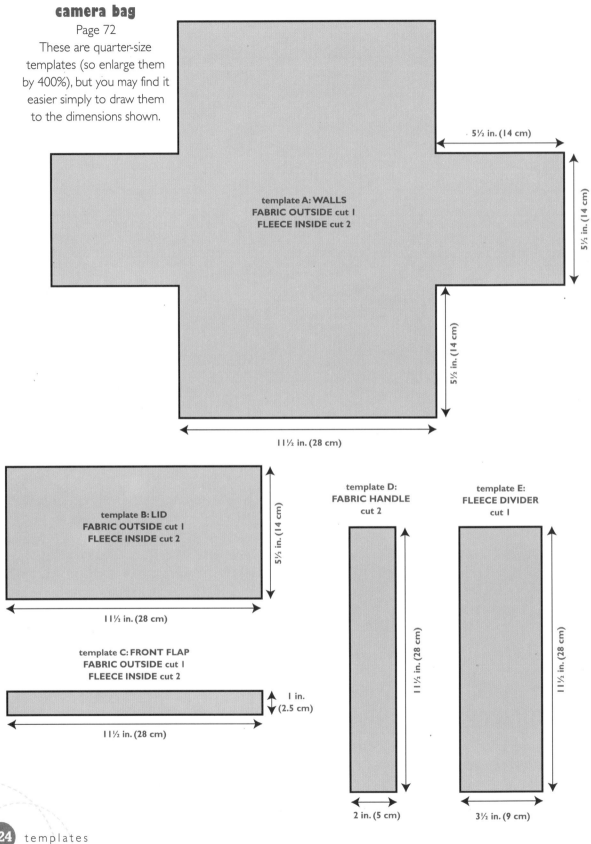

5½ in. (14 cm)

5½ in. (14 cm)

template A: WALLS
FABRIC OUTSIDE cut 1
FLEECE INSIDE cut 2

5½ in. (14 cm)

11½ in. (28 cm)

template B: LID
FABRIC OUTSIDE cut 1
FLEECE INSIDE cut 2

5½ in. (14 cm)

11½ in. (28 cm)

template C: FRONT FLAP
FABRIC OUTSIDE cut 1
FLEECE INSIDE cut 2

1 in. (2.5 cm)

11½ in. (28 cm)

template D:
FABRIC HANDLE
cut 2

11½ in. (28 cm)

2 in. (5 cm)

template E:
FLEECE DIVIDER
cut 1

11½ in. (28 cm)

3½ in. (9 cm)

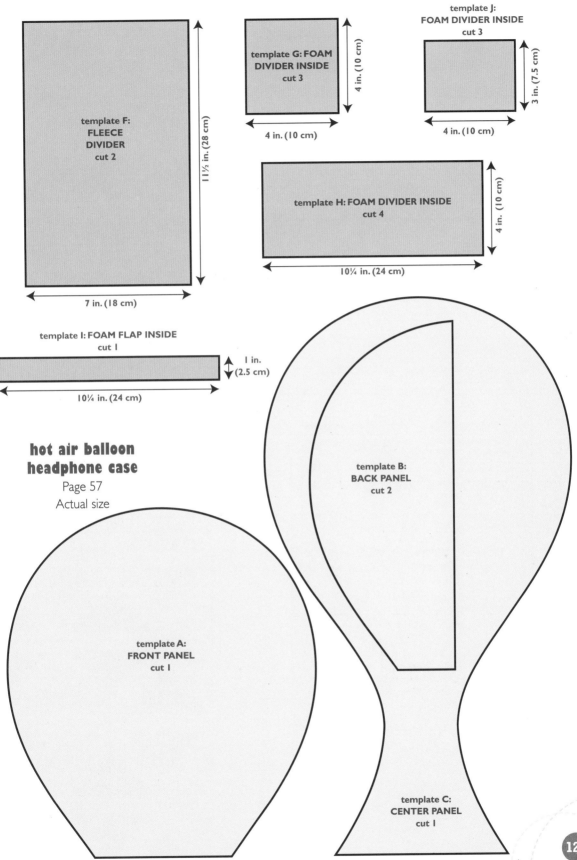

template F:
**FLEECE
DIVIDER**
cut 2

11½ in. (28 cm)

7 in. (18 cm)

template G: FOAM
DIVIDER INSIDE
cut 3

4 in. (10 cm)

4 in. (10 cm)

template J:
FOAM DIVIDER INSIDE
cut 3

3 in. (7.5 cm)

4 in. (10 cm)

template H: FOAM DIVIDER INSIDE
cut 4

4 in. (10 cm)

10¼ in. (24 cm)

template I: FOAM FLAP INSIDE
cut 1

1 in.
(2.5 cm)

10¼ in. (24 cm)

hot air balloon
headphone case
Page 57
Actual size

template B:
BACK PANEL
cut 2

template A:
FRONT PANEL
cut 1

template C:
CENTER PANEL
cut 1

DOUBLE MUG
cut 1

cup of tea
e-reader case
Page 91
Quarter-size
templates—enlarge
by 400%

TEA BAG
cut 2

MUG WINDOW
cut 1

laser cut phone case
Page 96
Actual size for an iPhone 5s

cross stitch
phone case
Page 94

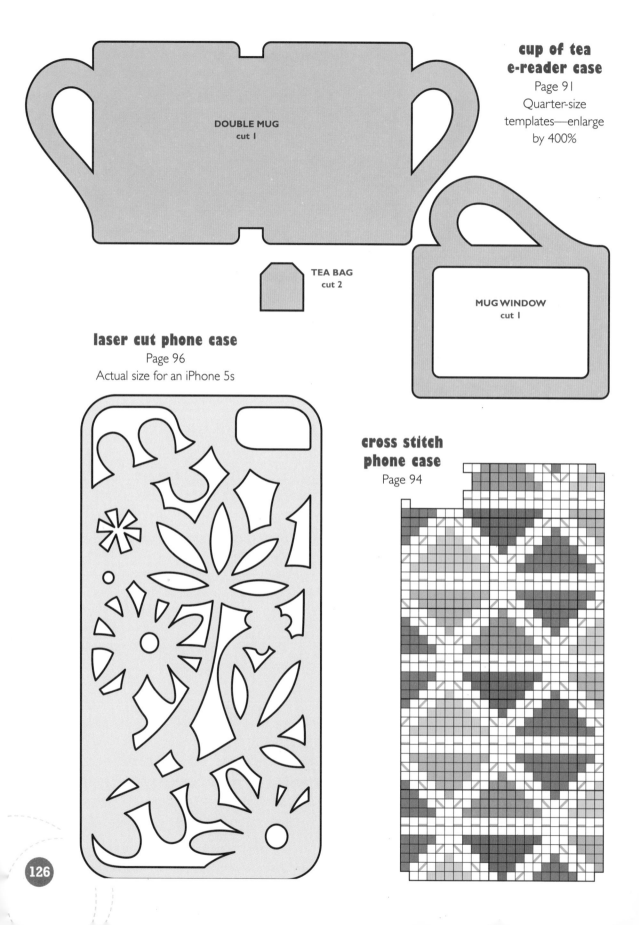

popsicle phone case

Page 104

Half-size templates—enlarge by 200%

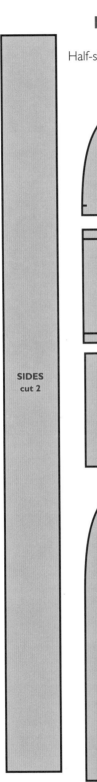

TOP PIECE
cut 2 in red fabric

MIDDLE PIECE
cut 2 in pink fabric

BOTTOM PIECE
cut 2 in orange fabric

SIDES
cut 2

WHOLE PIECE
cut 2 in orange fabric
cut 2 in felt

STICK
cut 1

suppliers

NORTH AMERICA

A.C. Moore
www.acmoore.com

Ace Hardware
www.acehardware.com

ALEX Toys
www.alextoys.com

Britex Fabrics
www.britexfabrics.com

Buy Fabrics
www.buyfabrics.com

The Charm Factory
www.charmfactory.com

Discount Fabrics USA
www.discountfabricsusacorp.com

Fabricland
www.fabricland.com

Hobby Lobby
www.hobbylobby.com

J & O Fabrics
www.jandofabrics.com

Jo-Ann Fabric and Craft Store
www.joann.com

Michaels
www.michaels.com

Purl Patchwork
www.purlsoho.com

UK

Abakhan Fabrics
www.abakhan.co.uk

Beads Direct Ltd
www.beadsdirect.co.uk

The Bead Shop
www.the-beadshop.co.uk

Beads Unlimited
www.beadsunlimited.co.uk

Coats Crafts
www.coatscrafts.co.uk

Hobby Craft
www.hobbycraft.co.uk

Homebase
www.homebase.co.uk

John Lewis
www.johnlewis.com

Josy Rose
www.josyrose.com

Kleins
www.kleins.co.uk

Liberty
www.liberty.co.uk

Rowan Yarns
www.knitrowan.com

index